THE ASIAN HOME KITCHEN

THE ASIAN HOME KITCHEN

FRESH, VIBRANT DISHES FROM KUALA LUMPUR TO KYOTO

LEEMEI TAN-BOISGILLOT

THE ASIAN HOME KITCHEN

Leemei Tan-Boisgillot

First published in the UK and USA in 2022 by
Nourish, an imprint of Watkins Media Limited
Unit 11, Shepperton House, 83–93 Shepperton Road
London N1 3DF

enquiries@nourishbooks.com

Recipes in this book have been previously published in
Lemongrass and Ginger by Leemei Tan-Boisgillot.

Managing Editor: Daniel Culver
Commissioning Editor: Ella Chappell
Editors: Camilla Davis and Josephine Bonde
Photography Art Director: Manisha Patel
Cover Design: Glen Wilkins
Art Director: Karen Smith
Design: Alice Claire Coleman
Illustrations: Alice Claire Coleman
Production: Uzma Taj
Commissioned Photography: Yuki Sugiura
Food Stylist: Aya Nishimura
Prop Stylist: Wei Tang

A CIP record for this book is available from the British Library

ISBN: 978-1-84899-408-9 (Hardback)
ISBN: 978-1-84899-409-6 (eBook)

10 9 8 7 6 5 4 3 2 1

Typeset in Brandon Grotesque
Printed in China

PUBLISHER'S NOTE:

While every care has been taken in compiling the
recipes for this book, Watkins Media Limited, or any
other persons who have been involved in working on this
publication, cannot accept responsibility for any errors
or omissions, inadvertent or not, that may be found in
the recipes or text, nor for any problems that may arise
as a result of preparing one of these recipes. If you are
pregnant or breastfeeding or have any special dietary
requirements or medical conditions, it is advisable to
consult a medical professional before following any of
the recipes contained in this book.

NOTES ON THE RECIPES:

Unless otherwise stated:
Use medium fruit and vegetables
Use medium (US large) organic or free-range eggs
Use fresh herbs, spices and chillies
Use granulated sugar (Americans can use ordinary
granulated sugar when caster sugar is specified)
Do not mix metric, imperial and US cup measurements:
   1 tsp = 5ml 1 tbsp = 15ml 1 cup = 240ml

DEDICATION

This book is dedicated to my mum, dad, family,

Arnaud, Nelly, Azma and Kristin.

contents

WELCOME TO MY KITCHEN

Home for me is Kedah in the northwestern state of Peninsula Malaysia where I grew up with my mum, dad, big sister and little brother. Picturesque, complete with lush paddy fields and dotted with kampungs (villages), the Kedah region is the 'Rice Bowl of Malaysia', producing more than half of Malaysia's rice supply.

Malaysia is a society where many diverse food cultures mix, so as I grew up, not only did I have the opportunity to eat many different foods but also I was encouraged by my parents to be bold and adventurous with what I ate. Delicious foods of all kinds were available to us in abundance, and right on our doorstep.

I grew up in a town where the main street was lined on both sides with a collection of shops and homes, and this is where we lived. Dad ran his retail business downstairs, we lived upstairs, and in our large backyard my mum grew chilli bushes, pandan plants and mango, papaya and calamansi (a type of citrus fruit) trees. We also raised free-range chickens.

Serving fresh, healthy and scrumptious meals to her family was important to my mum, and each day after we left for school she would make her way to the nearby markets to source the freshest ingredients to use when cooking our dinner. Because Friday was the first day of the weekend in Kedah State it meant I could join Mum at the markets. After what seemed like years of nagging her to let me come along, my first outing to the markets was a real adventure. One hand clinging onto my small straw bag and the other holding onto Mum's hand, I was mesmerized by the sounds, sights and smells. Traders and farmers vying for each customer's business; displays of amazing fresh fruits and vegetables; and massive boxes of crushed ice covering fresh seafood and fish shipped in daily from the two main shipping ports – Kuala Perlis and Kuala Kedah. I found it captivating, but equally as exciting for me was watching Mum turn all the wonderful fresh produce into amazing food. It was never a chore for me to get involved in the kitchen; I was a willing volunteer, taking on any task Mum felt confident I could cope with.

MUM'S LITTLE HELPER

Those early years in the kitchen – learning about different fresh roots, spices and other important ingredients in an Asian kitchen; helping with the chopping, grinding, pounding and slicing; and observing my mum gutting fish and preparing fresh poultry before cooking – are all experiences that have definitely formed my appreciation of fresh produce and my love of creating new dishes. Food was such an important part of my upbringing, and it wasn't until quite a few years later that I understood just how priceless this time was. Even though I was a very willing helper, there were times when I moaned about how the chores given to me were all related to food preparation: 'Why can't I cook a dish?', I would ask. The response was always the same, 'You have plenty to learn before I let you handle the wok.' I would pull a long and sulky face, not realizing that Mum wanted me to have a solid base in cooking. Back then, I could only observe how to do proper stir-frying, braising and steaming, but now I realize just how clever and insightful Mum was.

MY FORMATIVE YEARS

After I finished high school, I went to a college in Kuala Lumpur, and during this time, eating out became part of my lifestyle. There were street food hawkers almost at every corner, and it didn't take me long to get enthusiastic about the food scene. Along with eating street food, I used to eat regularly at restaurants, so I got to experience many different cuisines from around the world, further fuelling my interest in food. But there is something quite special about home-cooking, and I had always been pampered with Mum's. Luckily for me I had a wonderful landlady who was both kind and a very good cook. Mrs Seow often spoiled me with her home cooking. I will always remember fondly how on hot, humid days she would treat me to a traditional soupy dessert to help cool me down. Another lip-smacking, simple yet flavoursome dish that she prepared was Claypot Chicken Rice (*see page 104*). Her secret was to use a free-range chicken and to be bold with seasoning.

From Kuala Lumpur I moved to Perth, Australia, for two years to complete my university degree. Leaving my home and my family was very hard, but I was embarking on a new adventure and I was with a group of friends. This period turned out to be one of those important milestones in my life – it was also where my cooking skills were put to the test.

I shared a house with three friends: Peh-Ling, who was not confident in her cooking skills, so she was in charge of chopping the vegetables; Huey-Mein, who cooked a little, but everything looked dark and tasted sweet, as she is very fond of dark and sweet soy sauce; and there was Cathy, who like me had had a lot more hands-on experience in the kitchen. It was Cathy and I who ended up cooking most of the time.

As in my parents' house, we would always sit down to a bowl of fluffy white rice, which we would eat with a few different meat, fish and vegetable dishes, all nicely presented at the centre of the table – fresh and simple; fragrant and warm; delicious and healthy. I have many fond memories of this time, and quite recently Cathy and I were reminiscing about our mealtime moments when she suddenly paused and exclaimed, 'Never once did it cross anyone's mind to start dinner without everyone being home!' And it was our home away from home, a house filled with warmth and laughter. During those few years, cooking without any guidance from Mum, I learned to improvise, and this made me a keener and more confident cook.

LIVING IN LONDON

From Perth I returned to Kuala Lumpur to work, then, about seven years ago, I decided to take a sabbatical and pursued my dream to travel and experience more of the amazing world we live in. I headed for London. My first year in London flew by. I cooked more than I used to back in Malaysia, and my weekly telephone conversations with Mum were never without a discussion of food of some kind. There was also lots of 'How do you...?', 'Do you remember that dish that you made...?' and 'You know the spice paste that was freshly ground – how much of each ingredient do I use?' It was during this year that I realized just how much I had taken for granted during the cooking sessions in my parents' kitchen, and just how infectious Mum's enthusiasm had been!

It was during my second year in London, after I met my now fiancé, Arnaud, that the next stage of my food journey started. Along with our shared passion for food, we both love travelling, and Arnaud being French meant we made many trips to France. Slowly I was introduced to a different style of cooking from the many different regions of France, and new and amazing ingredients that were so different from those we use in Malaysia.

Arnaud's mother, Nelly, also loves cooking and enjoys good food, and for her, as it is for me, cooking is relaxing, therapeutic and never a chore. When I first met Nelly, I didn't speak French, nor she Mandarin or English, and it was food that helped us to connect with each other. Nelly, like my mum, is one of the best role models. Her impeccable skills inspire me, and I love her home cooking. It was meeting Arnaud and then Nelly that got me wondering, 'Is working with food my destiny?'

Travelling with Arnaud to the different regions in France and to many different countries, experiencing the wonderful diversity of culture and styles of cooking, has greatly influenced my own cooking. From each place I visit, I come away with a handful of recipes and a new appreciation of what authentic cooking means, inspiring me to learn new techniques and to develop my own style with an increasingly more international and modern flavour.

One life-changing experience was my visit to Tsukiji fish market in Tokyo, which gave me an insight into the importance of eating top-quality and fresh ingredients and preparing food simply. When you cook with fresh produce, you can turn a good dish into something that is exceptionally tasty, even when using the simplest cooking techniques. Nothing is more amazing than eating the freshest tuna sashimi, sliced in a particular way, which practically melts in your mouth. Even eating a freshly made bowl of the humble soba noodles, can bring about beaming, satisfied faces. At Tsukiji fish market, and generally when travelling through Japan, I learned so much about the importance of the words 'practical, simple, healthy and delicious' when it comes to cooking and food, and this is now central to my style of cooking – and a great example of this is my Soy & Mirin Tuna on Soba Noodles (*see page 38*).

Simplicity lets the food speak for itself. If ever asked what is the most memorable dish I ate when travelling somewhere specific, my answer seems always to be something that was prepared in home-cooking style – simply presented yet bursting with flavour. And when I get home and recreate these dishes in my own kitchen, I get great satisfaction from this approach.

I remember a particular experience when I was in Vietnam that instilled in me, and reassured me, that in the kitchen patience is a virtue. (And now I pay even more attention to how soup stock tastes and looks.) I watched an amazing lady in her 60s start her day at 4am to prepare the stock for her version of Vietnamese Chicken Noodle Soup (*see page 160*) that she later sold on her food stall. Onions and ginger were toasted until slightly charred before adding them to the water – along with star anise, cinnamon sticks, cloves and chicken carcasses – to make a fresh, rich stock.

Over the lowest heat possible, she left the ingredients to simmer ever so gently for hours, so as to avoid any cloudiness. The result was the most delicious, deep and flavoursome stock – with a hint of liquorice, cloves, onions and ginger. That, for me, is the result of patience and passion in cooking, which then brings warmth and happiness to those people who get to enjoy the meal.

Travelling has given me the incredible opportunity to immerse myself in learning about local foods and a country's culture. And I have had many fantastic and special experiences, when I have spent time really talking with local people to understand their culture, which, especially in Asian countries, has often evolved through food and, in particular, spice trading.

These conversations and observations have made me realize just how important, if not essential, it is to preserve the authenticity of recipes however much you adapt and modernize them. And this realization was in part the impetus behind starting my food and travel blog, My Cooking Hut, in 2007. I wanted to do my bit to spread the love of food, and its heritage, to other people all around the world.

MY COOKING HUT

For me, my blog is not only a way to record my food and travel experiences, but also a way to share and reminisce with fellow food and travel enthusiasts. Food is a wonderful way to bond people together, and through the world of blogging I have connected with so many fantastic, like-minded people from many different cultures and parts of the world.

It may only be a small contribution, but I hope that sharing my passion, knowledge and skills will inspire an interest in food and the origin of different dishes in people of all ages, and help them to appreciate just how closely related food and the lifestyles we live are.

Stepping into the food blogging world may not have been planned, but it has given me a better insight into many different cuisines and it has allowed me to explore my own talents and interests. It was through writing and talking about food that led me to food photography and styling. Never before had I appreciated the potential I showed in these areas, and as each day passes and I further submerge myself in my blog work, my passion grows stronger. Photography has enabled me to look at things differently and not only capture the beauty of food but appreciate some of the amazing scenery that God has blessed our world with.

What keeps me going is the encouragement that I receive from the loyal readers of my blog. Every day I am touched by the sweet and kind words I receive. I am so thankful for them, and it is this appreciation that makes me even more determined to produce and share beautiful recipes and photography.

AU REVOIR, LONDON!

After a decade, I bid farewell to London with a heavy heart. I remember the first time I landed at Heathrow Airport, there were so many unknowns, but I was very excited to explore this new phase of my life! I never thought I would spend so long living in this wonderful city. I was mesmerized by its people, architecture, culture, food scenes…

London will always have a special place in my heart – the opportunities it brought me; all the wonderful places I travelled to while living there; the countless number of times dining out at different restaurants; all the wonderful friends that I made over the years – and how food brought us together!

It moulded me into a different but better person, allowing me to look at things from different perspectives, including my way of cooking.

OUR NEW ADVENTURES BEGAN

We first visited Hong Kong back in 2015. Hong Kong is also known as 'Fragrant Harbour' – the direct phonetic translation of the city's Cantonese name 香港 (Heung Gong).

Hong Kong earned this nickname as a result of its important involvement in an ancient trade of fragrant incense. Our short stay in Hong Kong allowed us to get a bit of a flavour of the city. We took away some good memories and didn't know if we would visit again in the future, as it was just a stopover before we flew on to another destination in Asia.

'…we are currently cruising at an altitude of 10,600 metres at an airspeed of 650km per hour…'. We were halfway through the journey heading to the East, comfortably settled in our spacious seats and being pampered with a few glasses of Champagne before and after our in-flight dinner.

Had the short stopover trip to Hong Kong in 2015 prepared me in advance? This time we were heading to the same destination but for a different purpose – we had literally packed up everything in London to move to the Pearl of the Orient. It seemed unreal. It wasn't part of our plan, but a great opportunity had come along for us to live in Asia, which was a fascinating idea to my husband. My imagination began to run wild – I tried to think of all the possibilities and unexpected things that we might experience in order to get myself mentally and culturally prepared.

'Ladies and gentlemen. Welcome to Hong Kong International Airport. The temperature is 20°C…'.

It's hard to believe that we left London more than seven years ago and began our new adventure in Hong Kong.

LIVING IN HONG KONG

You would have thought any facts about Hong Kong should be within my fingertips. Well, they are to a certain extent, and although it's not a big country, one area can be quite different from another.

We have lived in Hong Kong Island, Kowloon, Lantau Island and New Territories within the last seven years! Yes, we have moved quite a bit! It's without a doubt that life has evolved during this period and we have different priorities now.

Yau Ma Tei in Kowloon is very authentic. It's chaotic and busy. An early morning stroll before dawn to the local wet market reminded me of when I was young, accompanying my mum to the 'pasar' (which means market in Malay). The wet market shared some similar characteristics to the ones in Malaysia – stalls set up along the roads selling different things, from fresh produce to daily storecupboard essentials.

I made a pit stop at a 'char chaan teng' (which literally means tea restaurant). These casual local restaurants became popular during the British colonial era to offer Western-style dishes with a Hong Kong twist at a fraction of the price of British-style afternoon tea. They offer an extensive selection of dishes ranging from sandwiches to rice meals, desserts and drinks.

One of my all-time favourite drinks is the Hong Kong-style milk tea, which is stronger, sweeter and creamier than an average cup of black tea served with a dash of milk. It can be enjoyed hot, or served cold with ice. Accompanying my drink was a savoury breakfast of macaroni in clear broth topped with a slice of ham and a fried egg (*see page* 69) and this is a perfect example of where East meets West; it's a very classic Hong Kong breakfast dish, which is indispensable for many Hong Kongers.

MY LOVE FOR TRAVELLING CONTINUED

Hong Kong is very strategically located, which means travelling within the region is very convenient. Multiple flights touching down and taking off are common scenes at one of the busiest airports in Asia. So there was no excuse not to tick a few destinations off our to-visit list and to see my family in Malaysia, at just a 3-hour flight away.

Within an hour of travelling by high-speed train from Hong Kong, it brought us to Guangzhou in Guangdong province, which is the heart and soul of Cantonese cuisine. Dim Sum dishes such as steamed prawn dumplings (*see page* 74) were abundant, delicious and cheap.

BBQ pork (*see page* 57) is another staple and popular dish from the region of Guangdong. Roasted meats are locally known as 'siu mei' (燒味) – the generic Cantonese name for meats roasted in a large rotisserie oven.

One of our memorable trips was to the Philippines – even though it was just a little over a two-hour flight to Manila, getting to the final destination involved another domestic flight, then a boat and finally a car transfer. The bumpy ride on the not-so-well-treated road wasn't much fun with small kids. I felt deflated after a whole day of travel.

Then, I felt a sudden sense of relaxation when we were welcomed by the wonderful shades of blue and turquoise from the endless ocean view. Contrasting with the blue were the fine, white silica sands on Panglao Island. Though feeling exhausted, I ordered a dish that I hadn't tasted for a while (in fact, since I first tried it) – Prawn & Tamarind Soup (*see page 87*). My taste buds reminded me of some lovely familiar ingredients and flavours. It couldn't have been served in a better place with a picture-perfect ocean backdrop, the warm sea breeze gently blowing through my fluffy hair, the warmth of the sun on my skin and the sweet smell of the salty sea air.

THE ASIAN HOME KITCHEN

Fast forward to the present day again... It feels as if it was just yesterday that I wrote the first edition of this book, *Lemongrass and Ginger*. I am chuffed to have this opportunity to update my original book, adding some new recipes to the different chapters that I feel are the continuation of those that came before. I trust they will bring you some new inspiration, happiness and comfort during the tough times we are all living through.

Being able to continue reminiscing about my travel and food experiences since living in London has been a blessing. Even though I wasn't using the same keyboard and screen, my passion for food remains just as strong as it ever was. Although certain perspectives in life have enhanced and reinforced my way and style of cooking, the principle remains the same, which is to strike a balance of flavours and achieve a harmonious dish each time.

All the recipes in this book, both new and old, pay homage to all the people and places that have inspired me. I am amazed by just how far my food journey has taken me since that first trip to the market with Mum. It has been, if truth be told, almost unbelievable. As I've sat in front of my computer screen typing away, so many vivid images have popped back into my mind that I can almost smell and taste the food, hear the banter and laughter, and feel the joy of sharing these moments with friends, family and new-found, food-loving enthusiasts. Being able to bring these experiences to life in my kitchen, and now in this book for you to cook and enjoy, is incredibly rewarding; to have this opportunity to show you just how tasty, rich and flavoursome authentic Asian cooking is – and how easy it is to prepare at home.

The recipes in this book are my take on wonderful, classic recipes of Asia. Many of them use modern ingredients and equipment – and different, more approachable techniques. They include recipes for dishes I have tasted during my travels that stand out in my memory. There are some that have been handed down from my family and others that were inspired by meals I enjoyed with people I've met or have eaten with family and friends.

As you flip through the book and read the recipes, you will discover, as I have, the significant differences in dishes from one country to the next, despite the countries bordering one another, such as China and India; or, even though two countries are far apart, incredible similarities between the ingredients and spices, as in Malaysian and Indian cuisines. There are so many different types of delicious Asian foods with amazing flavours and wonderful ranges of tastes, and the recipes I've included within each chapter have been chosen specifically so you can experience the diversity of Asian food.

When writing and compiling the recipes, it was important to me that they accurately reflect the flavours and nuances of the different countries, and to do this, a lot of fresh spices are used. Within the Basics section of the book, you will find 20 spice pastes (*see pages 226–231*) that are so easy to make, you will never again need to buy the ready-made versions. Using either a food processor or mortar and pestle, you can grind up fresh spice pastes in just a few minutes. Each paste recipe makes enough for one recipe or a meal for four people, but can easily be doubled, tripled, etc., and can also be stored in the refrigerator for up to one week.

No matter which Asian cuisine you are cooking, the balance of flavours is very important. There is no secret to making the most perfect and tastiest dish – it all lies in the tasting and balancing of flavours. So, when cooking my recipes, or if you are taking inspiration from them to create your own, taste, taste and taste again while you are cooking. This is an important Asian cooking technique that I guarantee will help you to achieve a harmony of flavours in every dish you cook.

Another important tip, as mentioned before, is to use the freshest ingredients possible. And if you have a well-stocked storecupboard, with all the condiments essential to Asian cooking, such as light soy sauce, dark soy sauce, sweet soy sauce, fish sauce, Chinese rice wine, cooking sake, mirin and sesame oil, you can create healthy and tasty Asian food at home with ease.

I live to eat, and love to eat, and I know this will never change. I hope when you are reading and using my book you will be inspired and I manage to set off a similar passion for good, fresh food.

Please do make a list of recipes 'to make and to try', as the kitchen is probably now an even more important and busy part of your life, not only a place to make delicious food, but somewhere that is the very heart and soul of your home. Trust your instincts, keep your passion and confidence and I am sure each dish you make will bring a smile to everyone's face.

Thai Beef Padand Curry. Page 146

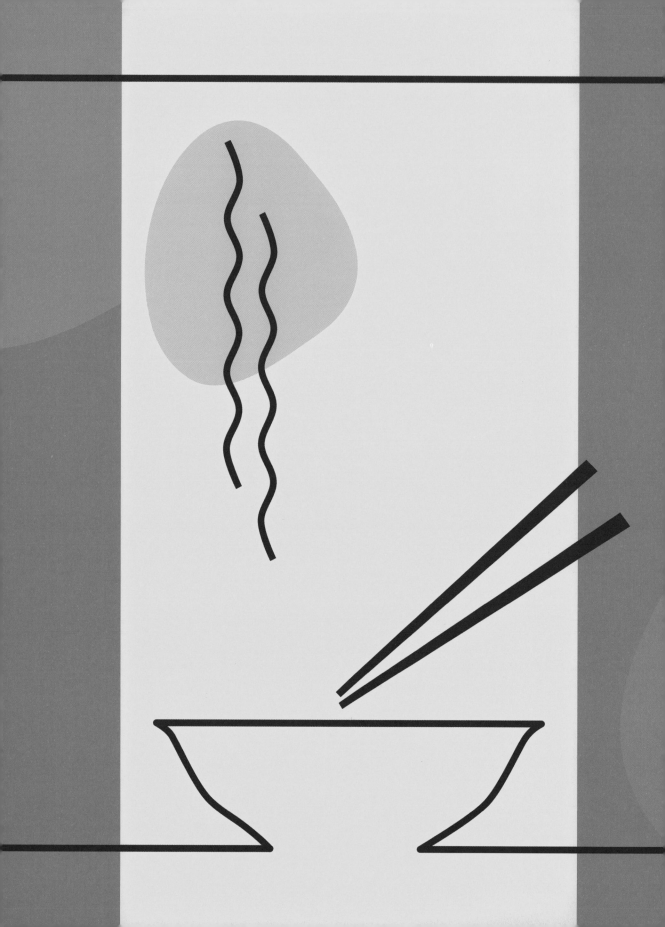

JAPAN & KOREA

In contrast to the spiciness of Korean and other Asian foods, Japanese cuisine is mild in flavour with sweetness and saltiness as the key tastes. It is simple, light and elegant, and is cooked using the best-quality and freshest ingredients available. In Japanese cooking, there is an emphasis on the purity of the natural ingredient and eating seasonally. Key ingredients used are shoyu, Japanese soy sauce; mirin, a sweetened sake; rice wine vinegar; and miso, a fermented bean paste, which is also an ingredient used to make Japanese stock. Rice is also an important part of Japanese meals, and is the base ingredient of many favourite dishes, including Sea Bream Nigirizushi (*see page 33*) and Tempura Prawn Temaki (*see page 37*).

Korean food is largely rice- and noodle-based, and because of the liberal use of Korean hot red chilli pepper and hot pepper paste is very much associated with piquancy. Other key ingredients used in Korean cooking are soy sauce, garlic, ginger, spring onions, sesame oil and toasted sesame seeds, and nearly all meals are served with Kimchi, a Korean pickle most commonly made with cabbage (the use of pak choi – *see page 46* – is my tweak on the classic). There is an abundance of seafood in Korean cooking, and pork and chicken are often eaten, but beef is by far the most popular meat, which is used in dishes such as Bibimbap (*see page 30*) and Sesame Barbecued Beef (*see page 32*).

SERVES **4**
PREPARATION TIME **25 minutes,**
    plus 25 minutes
    marinating time
COOKING TIME **15–20 minutes,**
    plus cooking the rice

150ml/5fl oz/scant ⅔ cup
    mirin
100ml/3½fl oz/generous
    ⅓ cup shoyu
2 tbsp sake
2 tbsp granulated sugar
1cm/½in piece of fresh
    ginger, peeled and finely
    grated, pulp discarded,
    reserving the juice
4 chicken legs, skin on and
    deboned (*see page 239*)
1 tbsp sesame seeds
½ recipe quantity Boiled
    Short-Grain Rice (*see
    page 237*)
400g/14oz baby leaf spinach
1 tbsp sunflower oil
250g/9oz cherry tomatoes
sea salt

CHICKEN TERIYAKI & ONIGIRI BENTO

Delicious, healthy and convenient is how I describe a bento. A simple packed lunch that consists of vegetables, meat or fish and rice. There are many variations of bento, and you can include anything you like – not just what I've selected here.

1 Put the mirin, shoyu, sake, sugar and ginger juice in a bowl. Mix until the sugar is dissolved, then add the chicken legs and coat well in the liquid. Cover with cling film/plastic wrap and leave to marinate in the refrigerator for about 25 minutes.

2 Meanwhile, heat a frying pan over a medium-high heat, then add the sesame seeds and dry-fry for a few minutes until the seeds begin to pop. Tip onto a plate and leave to one side.

3 Divide the warm, boiled rice into 8 equal portions. Moisten your hands to stop the rice sticking to them and scoop up a portion of rice. Shape it into a ball, then slightly flatten and sprinkle over the toasted sesame seeds. Repeat with the remaining portions of rice and leave to one side.

4 Bring a saucepan of salted water to the boil, add the spinach and cook for about 30 seconds. Drain and refresh the spinach under running cold water. Squeeze out any excess liquid and pat dry with paper towels. Divide into 4 equal portions, then shape each portion into 3 small balls. Leave to one side.

5 Heat the oil in a large saucepan over a medium-high heat. Add the chicken pieces, skin-side down, and cook for 5–6 minutes on each side until golden brown and the chicken is cooked through. Pour in the marinade and bring to the boil for a few seconds, then reduce the heat to medium and continue to cook the chicken until the sauce starts to thicken.

6 Remove from the heat and cut the chicken into bite-size slices. To assemble, divide the rice portions, spinach balls, chicken and cherry tomatoes into each bento or lunch box.

KORean FRIED CHICKen

SERVES **4**
PREPARATION TIME **20 minutes**
COOKING TIME **about 1 hour**

100g/3½oz/heaped ¾ cup
  plain/all-purpose flour, plus
  extra for dusting
3 tbsp cornflour/cornstarch
4 tbsp light soy sauce
1 tbsp granulated sugar
2 tbsp honey
1 tbsp sesame oil
4 garlic cloves, finely
  chopped
1cm/½in piece of fresh
  ginger, peeled and finely
  chopped
2 tbsp sesame seeds
500ml/17fl oz/2 cups
  sunflower oil, for
  deep-frying
1kg/2lb 4oz chicken wings

TO SERVE
1 recipe quantity Boiled
  Long-Grain Rice (*see
  page 237*)

A few years ago in New York, I stopped by a popular Korean eatery that is most famous for one dish – Double-Fried Chicken. That doesn't sound so sensational, right? I took my first bite from the chicken wing and was left speechless. Really crispy skin glazed with a soy sauce mixture. Amazing! I just wanted to keep eating and eating. Here I've recreated the recipe with the addition of sesame seeds for extra crunch.

1 Sift the plain flour and cornflour into a bowl, then gradually mix in 200ml/7fl oz/scant 1 cup water to form a batter and leave to one side.

2 In a small saucepan over a medium-high heat, add the soy sauce, sugar, honey, sesame oil, garlic, ginger and 1 tablespoon water. Bring to a gentle boil, then reduce the heat to low and simmer for 10 minutes until the mixture starts to thicken. Remove from the heat, strain over a large bowl and leave to one side.

3 Meanwhile, heat a frying pan over a medium-high heat, then add the sesame seeds and dry-fry for a few minutes until the seeds begin to pop. Tip onto a plate and leave to one side.

4 Heat the sunflower oil in a deep, heavy-based saucepan to 180°C/ 350°F or until a small piece of bread turns brown in 15 seconds. Lightly dust the chicken wings with flour, then coat with the batter and gently slide into the oil. Fry the wings in 2 or 3 batches for 10–15 minutes per batch until lightly golden brown, then remove from the oil, using a slotted spoon, and drain on paper towels. Avoid overcrowding the saucepan, as this will lower the temperature of the oil.

5 Let the chicken wings cool for 5 minutes and bring the heat back to 180°C/350°F. Re-fry the chicken in batches for a further 2 minutes per batch, or until golden brown and crisp, then remove from the oil and drain well on paper towels. Put the chicken pieces in the large bowl with the soy sauce mixture and toss until well coated. Sprinkle over the toasted sesame seeds and serve warm with boiled rice.

JAPANESE PORK & CABBAGE PANCAKES

Osaka in Japan is a heaven for food lovers, and when you stroll around its recognized area of gastronomy, Dotonburi, you are spoiled for choice. Restaurants line both sides of the streets. One of the specialities from Osaka is Okonomiyaki, a savoury pancake cooked on a griddle and topped with a Worcestershire-like sauce, mayonnaise and bonito. It is also very popular in the area of Hiroshima, but instead of mixing all the ingredients into the batter, Hiroshima-style Okonomiyaki is prepared by layering the ingredients.

MAKES **8 pancakes**
PREPARATION TIME **25 minutes**
COOKING TIME **about 1 hour 20 minutes**

220g/7¾oz/heaped 1¾ cups plain/all-purpose flour
½ tsp sea salt
1 tbsp sake
1 tbsp mirin
½ small white cabbage, core removed, rinsed and finely chopped
150g/5½oz minced/ground pork
14 raw, peeled large king prawns/jumbo shrimp, heads removed, with tails left on and deveined (*see page 241*)
2 spring onions, finely chopped
2 eggs, at room temperature
sunflower oil, for oiling
light mayonnaise, to serve
bonito flakes, to serve (optional)

SAUCE
3 tbsp tomato ketchup
4 tbsp Worcestershire sauce
2 tsp golden syrup
2 tsp shoyu

1 To make the sauce, put the tomato ketchup, Worcestershire sauce, golden syrup and shoyu in a small saucepan over a medium-high heat. Stir well and cook for 2–3 minutes until the sauce starts to thicken. Leave to one side to cool.

2 Sift the flour into a large mixing bowl, add 230ml/7¾fl oz/scant 1 cup water and mix well to form a thick batter. Stir in the salt, sake and mirin, then add the cabbage, pork, prawns and spring onions. Break in the eggs, mix until well combined and set aside.

3 Pour some oil into a large, heavy-based frying pan over a medium-high heat, then use paper towels to grease the pan evenly and soak up any excess oil. When the pan is hot, add 3–4 tablespoons of the mixture and flatten it into a 12cm/4½in disc. Cook for 8–10 minutes, then, using a spatula, flip over the okonomiyaki and cook the other side for 8–10 minutes until golden brown and crisp. Remove from the pan and keep warm while you make the remaining pancakes. If they will fit in the pan, cook 2 okonomiyaki at a time. Oil the pan again, as required.

4 Divide the okonomiyaki between individual serving plates, brush with the sauce and then top with a generous dollop of mayonnaise and a scattering of bonito flakes, if using. Serve hot.

JAPANESE BEEF STEW

SERVES 4–6
PREPARATION TIME **20 minutes,**
  plus making the Dashi
COOKING TIME **45 minutes**

80g/2¾oz sugar snap peas
1 tbsp sunflower oil
500g/1lb 2oz casserole
  steak, trimmed of fat and
  cut into bite-size pieces
1 onion, cut into wedges
3 carrots, cut into bite-size
  pieces
2 potatoes, quartered
1 parsnip, cut into bite-size
  pieces
250g/9oz daikon, quartered
½ recipe quantity Dashi
  (*see page 233*)
2 tbsp sake or rice wine
2 tbsp sugar
4 tbsp shoyu

TO SERVE
1 recipe quantity Boiled
  Long-Grain Rice (*see
  page 237*)

The Japanese absolutely love to eat beef cooked hotpot-style such as Nikujaga. The beef is very thinly sliced, stir-fried and then simmered with vegetables in a flavourful dashi. Here I suggest using beef topside or rump; however, for a truly sensational dish you could use wagyu beef. Originating in Japan, wagyu is now available worldwide. The fat is evenly distributed throughout the flesh and melts as the meat is cooked, giving it a soft and juicy texture and a rich flavour.

1 Prepare a bowl of ice-cold water and bring a saucepan of water to the boil. Add the sugar snap peas to the boiling water and blanch for 1–2 minutes. Drain, then put the sugar snaps into the iced water to stop the cooking process. Leave to one side.

2 Heat the oil in a frying pan or saucepan over a medium-high heat. Add the beef and cook, stirring occasionally, for 3 minutes until sealed and beginning to brown. Add the onion and cook for 2–3 minutes until soft and translucent, then add the carrots and cook for 3 minutes, or until almost tender.

3 Tip in the potatoes, parsnip, daikon, dashi, sake and sugar. Bring to the boil and then push the ingredients around the pan, making sure the vegetables are covered by the dashi. Reduce the heat to low, cover and simmer for 20 minutes. Add the shoyu and prepared sugar snap peas and cook, covered, for a further 5 minutes. Serve immediately with boiled rice.

SERVES 4
PREPARATION TIME **30 minutes,**
plus 25 minutes freezing
and soaking time
COOKING TIME **45 minutes**

200g/7oz beef fillet,
wrapped and semi-frozen
for 25 minutes (*see
page 242*)
2 tbsp sunflower oil
1 garlic clove, finely chopped
1 tbsp light soy sauce
6 dried shiitake mushrooms,
soaked, drained and cut
into thin strips (*see
page 242*)
1 tsp sesame oil
120g/4¼oz/generous 1 cup
bean sprouts
1 small carrot, cut into
matchsticks
1 courgette/zucchini, thinly
sliced
200g/7oz baby leaf spinach
4 eggs
1 recipe quantity Boiled
Short-Grain Rice
(*see page 237*)
freshly ground black pepper

TO SERVE
1 tbsp sesame seeds
Korean hot pepper paste

BIBIMBAP

'Bibim' in Korean means to mix and 'bap' means rice, so this dish literally means 'mixed rice'. There is a popular variation of Bibimbap – Dol Sot Bibimbap – where the cooked rice is spread over the base of a stone pot and becomes crunchy during cooking. The other cooked ingredients are arranged on the rice and then a raw egg is added just before serving and stirred into the rice to cook it.

1 Heat a frying pan over a medium-high heat, then add the sesame seeds and dry-fry for a few minutes until the seeds begin to pop. Tip onto a plate and leave to one side.

2 Remove the partially frozen beef from the freezer and unwrap the cling film/plastic wrap. Using a sharp knife, cut the beef against the grain into 3mm/⅛in-thick slices.

3 Heat 1 tablespoon of the sunflower oil in a frying pan over a medium-high heat. Add the garlic and stir-fry for 1 minute, then add the beef and stir-fry for 5–6 minutes until brown and cooked through. Add the soy sauce and season with pepper. Remove the beef from the pan and keep warm. Still over a medium-high heat, add the shiitake mushrooms to the pan and stir-fry for 2 minutes, then drizzle over the sesame oil. Remove the mushrooms from the pan, using a slotted spoon, leave to one side and keep warm. Repeat the same process, without adding the sesame oil, with the bean sprouts and then the carrot.

4 Meanwhile, steam the courgette for 5 minutes, or until soft, and leave to one side. Steam the spinach for 2–3 minutes until wilted, then drain, squeeze out any excess water and leave to one side.

5 Heat the remaining sunflower oil in a large frying pan over a medium heat and fry the eggs for about 3 minutes each – the yolks should still be runny. Meanwhile, gently warm the beef and vegetables in a separate frying pan.

6 To assemble, divide the warm cooked rice into serving bowls, then divide the beef and vegetables between the dishes. Put a fried egg in the centre of each bowl. Sprinkle over the toasted sesame seeds and serve immediately with the Korean hot pepper paste on the side.

SESAME BARBECUED BEEF

Bulgogi is one of two dishes (*see* Pak Choi Kimchi *on page 46 for the other*) that really stuck with me after my first visit to Korea. The beef was very thinly sliced and gently marinated, then served raw on a platter with vegetables for each guest to cook on a shared grill at the table. Keeping the delicious, clean flavours, here is a modern take on the traditional dish with everything cooked in a pan instead.

SERVES 4
PREPARATION TIME 15 minutes, plus 1 hour 25 minutes freezing and marinating time
COOKING TIME 20 minutes

500g/1lb 2oz rib-eye steak or sirloin, wrapped and semi-frozen for 25 minutes (*see page 242*)
3½ tbsp light soy sauce
2 tbsp granulated sugar
2 tbsp sesame oil
3 garlic cloves, finely chopped
1cm/½in piece of fresh ginger, peeled and finely chopped
1 onion, sliced
2 tbsp sesame seeds
1 tbsp sunflower oil
2 spring onions/scallions, finely chopped

TO SERVE
1 recipe quantity Boiled Long-Grain Rice (*see page 237*)

1 Remove the partially frozen beef from the freezer and unwrap the cling film/plastic wrap. Using a sharp knife, cut the beef against the grain into 3mm/⅛in slices, or even thinner if possible.
2 Put the beef in a large bowl with the soy sauce, sugar, sesame oil, garlic, ginger and onion and mix well. Cover with cling film/plastic wrap and leave to marinate in the refrigerator for about 1 hour.
3 Meanwhile, heat a frying pan over a medium-high heat, then add the sesame seeds and dry-fry for a few minutes until the seeds begin to pop. Tip onto a plate and leave to one side.
4 Heat the sunflower oil in a ridged griddle pan or heavy-based frying pan over a high heat. When the oil begins to smoke, add the marinated beef and cook for a few seconds before turning the heat down to medium-high. Spread out the meat in the pan, laying it as flat as possible so it cooks evenly. Cook for 10–15 minutes, turning occasionally, until the beef is browned and tender.
5 One minute before the end of cooking, add the spring onions. Sprinkle over the toasted sesame seeds and serve immediately with boiled rice.

SEA BREAM NIGIRIZUSHI

SERVES 4
PREPARATION TIME 15 minutes,
    plus cooking the rice

200g/7oz boneless, skinless
    sea bream or sea bass fillet
½ recipe quantity Boiled
    Short-Grain Rice, cooled
    (see page 237)
1 tsp wasabi

TO SERVE
wasabi
shoyu
Pickled Ginger (see
    page 236)

Nigirizushi is one of the most popular Japanese sushi, and is also called hand-formed sushi, because the rice is pressed and moulded into an oblong shape. I've used short-grain rice because it is readily available and gives a similar texture to sushi rice. It also takes less time to cook, which means these delicious morsels are quick to make. The blushing pink and thinly sliced pieces of sea bream are fresh and great in taste, although you can use other kinds of seafood.

1 Place the fish fillet horizontally to you on a chopping/cutting board. Angle the knife at 45° to the fillet and cut the fillet against the grain into slices of about 3cm/1¼in wide and 3–5mm/⅛–¼in thick.

2 Moisten your hands with water to avoid the rice sticking and scoop up about 1 tablespoon of rice with one hand. Put it in the palm of your other hand and shape the rice into a 5 x 2.5cm/2 x 1in oblong with rounded corners. Take a slice of the prepared sea bream in one hand and smear over a small amount of wasabi. Place the rice on top of the slice of fish, then gently press down on the rice to stick them together. Turn the nigirizushi over and press the top and the sides to make sure the fish is firmly in place. Continue until all the remaining rice and fish is used. Serve with wasabi, shoyu and pickled ginger.

Korean-style Makizushi

SERVES **4**
PREPARATION TIME **45 minutes,
plus 20 minutes cooling
time**
COOKING TIME **10 minutes, plus
cooking the rice**

4 tsp sesame seeds
1 recipe quantity Boiled
   Short-Grain Rice
   (*see page 237*)
2 tbsp sesame oil
4 nori sheets (20 x 18cm/
   8 x 7in)

FILLING
2 eggs
1 tsp sunflower oil
200g/7oz baby leaf spinach
½ carrot, cut into
   matchsticks
½ cucumber, halved
   lengthways, deseeded
   and cut into strips
12 crabsticks
fine sea salt

DIPPING SAUCE
2 tbsp light soy sauce
1 tbsp rice vinegar
generous 1 tbsp lemon juice

1 Heat a frying pan over a medium-high heat, then add the sesame seeds and dry-fry for a few minutes until the seeds begin to pop. Tip half the sesame seeds into a mini food processor and grind to a fine powder. Leave the other half of the sesame seeds to one side.

2 To make the dipping sauce, whisk all the ingredients together with the ground sesame seeds until well combined. Leave to one side.

3 Transfer the cooked rice to a large wooden bowl or a non-metal baking dish. Add the sesame oil and remaining toasted sesame seeds and gently fold through the rice using a spatula. Level the rice, cover with a damp dish towel and leave to cool to room temperature.

4 To make the filling, beat the eggs together with a pinch of fine salt in a small bowl. Pour the sunflower oil into a large, heavy-based frying pan over a medium-high heat, then use a paper towel to grease the pan evenly and soak up any excess oil. When the pan is hot, pour in the beaten eggs and turn the heat down to low. Cook the omelette for 3 minutes on each side until cooked through but not coloured. Leave to one side to cool, then cut into strips.

5 Meanwhile, bring a saucepan of salted water to the boil, add the spinach and cook for about 30 seconds. Drain and refresh under running cold water. Squeeze out any excess liquid and pat dry with paper towels. Leave to one side.

6 Cover a bamboo sushi mat with cling film/plastic wrap and put on a clean surface with a long side closest to you. Leaving a gap of about 2cm/¾in at the edge nearest to you, place a nori sheet, rough side up, on the mat. Moisten one of your hands to help stop the rice sticking to it, then scoop up one-quarter of the rice and spread it evenly over two-thirds of the nori sheet, leaving a small gap at each end. Place 4–6 strips of omelette, a small handful of spinach, 2–3 strips of carrot, 2–3 strips of cucumber and 3 crabsticks horizontally along the middle of the rice.

7 Bring up the bottom edge of the mat, fold it over the filling and then roll the nori up into a cylinder, pressing firmly at the same time to make sure the makizushi is tight and compact. Put a few kernels of cooked rice along the end of the nori sheet and press firmly to seal. Give the mat a final press to create a tight roll. Leave the roll to one side and cover with cling film/plastic wrap. Repeat to make 3 more rolls.

8 To finish, lightly moisten the blade of a sharp knife and cut each roll into 5 or 6 rounds. Serve with the dipping sauce.

TEMPURA PRAWN TEMAKI

MAKES **14**
PREPARATION TIME **1 hour 35 minutes**
COOKING TIME **1 hour, plus cooking the rice**

100g/3½oz/heaped ¾ cup plain/all-purpose flour, plus extra for dusting
2 tbsp cornflour/cornstarch
1 tsp baking powder
1 egg yolk
160ml/5¼fl oz/⅔ cup ice-cold sparkling water
3 tbsp sesame seeds
500ml/17fl oz/2 cups sunflower oil, for deep-frying
14 raw, peeled large king prawns/jumbo shrimp, heads removed, with tails left on and deveined (*see page 214*)
3 tbsp light mayonnaise
2 tbsp lemon juice
1 spring onion/scallion, green part only, finely chopped
7 nori sheets (20 x 18cm/ 8 x 7in), halved lengthways
1 recipe quantity Boiled Short-Grain Rice, cooled (*see page 237*)
1 small cucumber, quartered, deseeded and cut into strips
1 small carrot, cut into matchsticks
sea salt

TO SERVE
shoyu
wasabi paste (optional)

When I visit a Japanese restaurant, I always order Tempura and Temaki. Tempura is a dish of seafood or vegetables coated in a light batter, then deep-fried, and Temaki is a cone-like sushi that is pretty to look at and tasty to eat. I've created Tempura Prawn Temaki so that you can enjoy both of these delicious dishes in one!

1 Mix together the plain flour, cornflour and baking powder in a mixing bowl. In a separate bowl, lightly whisk together the egg yolk and add the sparkling water. Pour the egg mixture into the dry ingredients and lightly fold it through using a whisk. Don't overmix the batter – it should stay lumpy. Put the batter bowl into a larger bowl that is half filled with ice cubes to keep the batter cold at all times.

2 Heat a frying pan over a medium-high heat, then add the sesame seeds and dry-fry for a few minutes until the seeds begin to pop. Tip onto a plate and leave to one side.

3 Heat the oil in a deep, heavy-based saucepan to 170°C/325°F or until a small piece of bread turns brown in 20 seconds. Lightly coat each prawn in a little flour, shaking off the excess. Dip the prawn into the batter, then gently slide it into the oil. Fry 2–3 prawns at a time, each one for 2–3 minutes, or until a light golden brown. Remove the prawns, using a slotted spoon, and drain on paper towels. Repeat until all the prawns are cooked.

4 Combine the mayonnaise, lemon juice, spring onion and a pinch of salt in a small bowl. To assemble, place a nori sheet on a clean surface with the longest edge closest to you, rough side up. Moisten one of your hands with water, then scoop up about 2 heaped tablespoons of the rice. Spread the rice evenly over the half of the nori sheet closest to you, leaving the bottom corner free of rice also.

5 Spread 1–2 teaspoons of the mayonnaise mixture evenly over the rice and sprinkle over the toasted sesame seeds. Add 1 tempura prawn, 2–3 cucumber strips and 2–3 carrot strips diagonally on top of the rice. Fold the bottom corner of the nori over the ingredients to form a pointed end and then continue to roll to make a cone shape. Stick one or two rice kernels at the corner end and press firmly to seal. Continue until all the ingredients are used. Serve with shoyu, mixed with a little wasabi paste, if you like, for dipping.

SOY & MIRIN TUNA ON SOBA NOODLES

SERVES 4
PREPARATION TIME 15 minutes,
plus 35 minutes cooling
and marinating time
COOKING TIME 15 minutes, plus
cooking the noodles

400g/14oz skinless tuna
125ml/4fl oz/½ cup shoyu
100ml/3½fl oz/generous
⅓ cup mirin
1 tbsp granulated sugar
1cm/½in piece of fresh
ginger, peeled and finely
grated, pulp discarded,
reserving the juice
1 tbsp sesame seeds
1 tsp sunflower oil
350g/12oz cooked green tea
soba or buckwheat soba
noodles (*see page 239*)
1 spring onion/scallion, finely
chopped, to serve

Soba means 'buckwheat' in Japanese and there are two types of soba noodles – the normal dark brown noodle with the natural colour of buckwheat and the green-coloured 'green tea' soba. You can use either, but the green tea version looks very pretty and gives a fresher, lighter taste to the dish.

1 Bring a saucepan of water to the boil, then poach the tuna loin for 25–30 seconds to seal. Remove the tuna from the water, pat dry and transfer to a plate to cool for about 5 minutes.

2 Meanwhile, mix the shoyu, mirin, sugar and ginger juice in a large bowl. Add the seared tuna and thoroughly coat with the marinade. Cover with cling film/plastic wrap and leave to marinate in the refrigerator for 30 minutes.

3 Heat a frying pan over a medium-high heat, then add the sesame seeds and dry-fry for a few minutes until the seeds begin to pop. Tip onto a plate and leave to one side.

4 Remove the tuna from the marinade and strain the marinade into a small saucepan. Simmer the marinade over a medium heat for 2–3 minutes until slightly thickened. Remove from the heat and keep warm.

5 Heat the oil in a large frying pan over a high heat, then add the tuna and sear for 1–2 minutes on each side. The outer layer should be cooked and golden brown but the inside should remain raw – don't cook the tuna completely through. Transfer the tuna to a chopping/cutting board, angle a sharp knife at 45° to the surface and slice against the grain into 5mm/¼in strips.

6 Meanwhile, while the tuna is searing, bring another saucepan of water to the boil and plunge in the soba noodles for a few seconds to heat through. Drain and divide the noodles into deep soup bowls, then top with the tuna. Drizzle the reduced marinade over the tuna and sprinkle over the toasted sesame seeds and spring onion. Serve hot or cold.

CHICKEN & EGG RICE BOWL

Love chicken and egg? This dish gives you the best of both – simple ingredients, yet it brings so much comfort accompanied with fluffy rice. I really like how quick one can whip up this dish. It's definitely elegance in a bowl.

SERVES **4**
PREPARATION TIME **15 minutes,**
  plus making the dashi
COOKING TIME **20 minutes**

150ml/5fl oz/⅔ cup recipe
  quantity Dashi (*see page
  233*)
2 tbsp mirin
2 tbsp sake or rice wine
2 tbsp shoyu
2 tbsp granulated sugar
400g/14oz skinless,
  boneless chicken thighs,
  cut into bite-size pieces
1 onion, cut into wedges
4 eggs, lightly beaten
1 spring onion/scallion,
  finely chopped

TO SERVE
1 recipe quantity Boiled
  Short-Grain Rice (*see page
  237*)

1 Put the dashi, mirin, sake, shoyu and sugar in a bowl. Mix until the sugar is dissolved. Transfer to a frying pan set over a medium-high heat and bring to the boil.

2 Tip in the chicken pieces, spreading them out in the pan and laying them as flat as possible so the meat cooks evenly. Add the onion wedges over the chicken, then cover with the lid and cook over a medium heat for about 10 minutes, or until the chicken is cooked through.

3 Remove the lid and pour in the beaten egg to cover the chicken pieces, then sprinkle over the spring onion. Cook for about 1–2 minutes with the lid on. The egg texture should be slightly runny. Remove from the heat.

4 To assemble, divide the warm cooked rice into individual bowls, then divide the egg and chicken mixture equally between the portions of rice. Serve immediately.

korean spicy seafood noodle soup

SERVES 4–6
PREPARATION TIME 45 minutes to 1 hour, plus making the stock
COOKING TIME 30 minutes, plus cooking the noodles

1 tbsp sesame seeds
15g/½oz dried wakame
500g/1lb 2oz mussels, scrubbed and debearded
1 tbsp sunflower oil
1 onion, sliced
3 garlic cloves, finely chopped
1cm/½in piece of fresh ginger, peeled and finely chopped
4 dried shiitake mushrooms, soaked, drained and cut into thin strips (*see page 242*)
1 tbsp Korean red pepper powder or cayenne pepper
1 recipe quantity Chicken Stock (*see page 232*)
¼ Chinese cabbage, core removed and cut into bite-size pieces
1 tbsp light soy sauce
1 tbsp Chilli Oil (*see page 234*)
300g/10½oz raw, peeled large king prawns/jumbo shrimp, tails left on, deveined (*see page 241*)
400g/14oz squid, scored with a crisscross pattern and cut into bite-size pieces (*see page 241*)
500g/1lb 2oz cooked fresh fine egg noodles or 350g/12oz dried fine egg noodles (*see page 238*)
2 spring onions/scallions, finely chopped

1 Heat a frying pan over a medium-high heat, then add the sesame seeds and dry-fry for a few minutes until the seeds begin to pop. Tip onto a plate and leave to one side.

2 Soak the dried wakame in a small bowl in warm water for about 10 minutes until it rehydrates. Drain, rinse and leave to one side.

3 Tap any mussels that are only partly opened and discard any that don't shut. Put the mussels in a saucepan over a high heat and steam for 3–4 minutes, or until the shells open. Discard any that don't open fully. There is no need to add any additional liquid to the pan, as the mussels will release their own liquid to steam in. Remove the mussels from their shells and leave to one side.

4 Heat the sunflower oil in a large saucepan over a medium-high heat. Add the onion and cook for 2–3 minutes until soft and translucent, then add the garlic and ginger and cook for 2 minutes, or until fragrant. Add the shiitake mushrooms and Korean red pepper powder and cook, stirring continuously, for 1 minute. Remove from the heat and add the chicken stock.

5 Return the pan to the heat and bring the chicken stock to the boil. Add the Chinese cabbage and cook for 3–4 minutes until tender. Add the soy sauce and chilli oil and then add the prawns and squid. Bring to the boil for a few seconds, then reduce the heat to low, cover and simmer for 5–6 minutes, or until the prawns turn pink and are cooked through and the squid is tender. Three minutes before the end of cooking, add the mussels to heat through.

6 Divide the hot, cooked noodles into deep soup bowls, then spoon the prawns, squid, cabbage and mussels into the bowls.

7 Bring the chicken stock to a vigorous boil. Add the spring onions and prepared wakame to the bowls, then ladle in the piping hot stock. Sprinkle over the toasted sesame seeds and serve immediately.

SPICY KOREAN RICE CAKES

SERVES **4**
PREPARATION TIME **15 minutes,
 plus 10 minutes soaking
 time**
COOKING TIME **40 minutes**

½ tbsp sesame seeds
500g/1lb 2oz thawed frozen
 Korean cylinder-shaped
 rice cakes
1 small handful of dried
 anchovies
250g/9oz fish cakes, sliced
2 hard-boiled eggs, cooled,
 peeled and halved
 (optional)
2 spring onions/scallions,
 finely chopped

SAUCE
2 garlic cloves, finely
 chopped
2 tbsp light soy sauce
1 tsp granulated sugar
2 tbsp Korean hot pepper
 paste (gochujang)
1 tbsp Korean chilli flakes
 (gochugaru)
1 tsp sesame oil

These soft and chewy cylinder-shaped rice cakes drenched in bright red spicy sauce, known by their Korean name as *Tteokbokki*, are a very popular Korean street food that can be whipped up easily at home. *Tteokbokki*, literally meaning 'stir fried rice cakes', served with this slightly sweet and spicy sauce, provide a really tasty comfort food. You can adjust the spiciness to your liking by adding more *gochugaru* (Korean chilli flakes).

1 Heat a frying pan over a medium-high heat, then add the sesame seeds and dry-fry for a few minutes until the seeds begin to pop. Tip onto a plate and leave to one side.

2 Separate and rinse the rice cakes under running cold water, drain well and transfer to a large bowl. Cover the rice cakes with warm water and leave for about 10 minutes, or until softened. Drain and set aside.

3 To make the sauce, add all the ingredients to a bowl, mix until well combined and set aside.

4 Bring 1 litre/35fl oz/4¼ cups of water to the boil in a large pot or saucepan over a medium-high heat. Add the dried anchovies and reduce the heat to medium-low, then simmer for about 15–20 minutes. Using a slotted spoon, remove and discard the anchovies.

5 Bring the stock back to a gentle boil, stir in the sauce mixture and cook for about 5 minutes. Add the rice cakes and fish cakes, then cook for about 10 minutes, stirring occasionally, until the rice cakes become tender and the sauce is thickened.

6 Top with the boiled egg halves, if you like, and sprinkle over the toasted sesame seeds and spring onions. Serve hot.

Korean tofu stew

SERVES **4**
PREPARATION TIME **15 minutes**
COOKING TIME **20 minutes**

1 tbsp sunflower oil
200g/7oz pork fillet, sliced
2 garlic cloves, finely
  chopped
1 tbsp Korean chilli flakes
  (gochugaru)
2 tsp Korean hot pepper
  paste (gochujang)
80g/2¾oz kimchi, sliced
700g/1lb 9oz silken tofu,
  drained and cut into
  medium cubes
200g/7oz enoki mushrooms
2 spring onions/scallions,
  finely chopped
1 egg (optional)
fine sea salt

TO SERVE
1 recipe quantity Boiled
  Short-Grain Rice (*see
  page 237*)

It was a very snowy evening and really cold, so I layered myself with lots of warm clothes. Looking out of the window from my Gangnam hotel room there was a very beautiful winter scene. I braved myself and headed to a nearby small family restaurant just to satisfy my craving for *Sundubu-jjigae* or Korean tofu stew. It was such a delicious bowl of goodness made with simple, fresh ingredients, topped by the warmth of the lady who served me, which made it a really authentic and memorable experience. '*Jal meokkessumnida*,' I said, which is a way to show appreciation to the person who prepared the dish.

1 Heat the oil in a casserole pot over a medium-high heat. Tip in the pork and cook, stirring occasionally, for about 3 minutes. Add the garlic, chilli flakes, hot pepper paste and kimchi. Stir until well coated and cook for 5 minutes.
2 Pour in 500ml/17fl oz/2 cups of water and bring to the boil. Reduce the heat to medium-low, add the silken tofu and enoki mushrooms and simmer for about 5–10 minutes. Season with a pinch of salt and bring to a gentle boil.
3 Remove from the heat, sprinkle with the spring onions. If you like, crack an egg into the stew while it is still bubbling hot. Serve immediately with boiled rice.

MAKES 28
PREPARATION TIME about 1 hour,
   plus 1 hour marinating and
   resting time
COOKING TIME 10–20 minutes

175g/6oz white cabbage,
   halved and core removed
80g/2¾oz watercress,
   chopped
5 spring onions/scallions,
   finely chopped
270g/9½oz minced/ground
   pork
7 garlic cloves, finely
   chopped
2cm/¾in piece of fresh
   ginger, peeled and finely
   chopped
1 tbsp cornflour/cornstarch
1 tbsp sesame oil
3 tbsp shoyu
1 tbsp sake
1 tsp mirin
1 tsp granulated sugar
1–2 tbsp sunflower oil
freshly ground black pepper

GYOZA WRAPPERS
200g/7oz/scant 1⅔ cups
   plain/all-purpose flour, plus
   extra for dusting
sunflower oil, for oiling
sea salt

TO SERVE
shoyu
Chilli Oil (*see page 234 –
   optional*)

JAPANESE PORK DUMPLINGS

Growing up in a Chinese family meant that we often made and ate dumplings. I remember lovely times in the kitchen helping my mother to make the wrappers from scratch and prepping the ingredients. As time has passed, dumplings have evolved in my life and I have started using different ingredients such, as watercress instead of the usual cabbage, to make this dish explode with flavours.

1 Bring a large saucepan of water to the boil, add the cabbage leaves and blanch for 1 minute. Remove the leaves with kitchen tongs and plunge immediately into a bowl of ice-cold water to stop the cooking process. Drain, pat dry with paper towels, squeezing out as much water as possible, and then finely chop. Transfer to a large bowl and add the watercress and spring onions.

2 Mix together the pork, garlic, ginger, cornflour, sesame oil, shoyu, sake, mirin and sugar in a large bowl until well combined and then season with pepper. Add the cabbage and watercress mix and stir to combine. Cover with cling film/plastic wrap and leave to marinate in the refrigerator for 1 hour.

3 Meanwhile, to make the gyoza wrappers, put the flour and a pinch of salt in a large mixing bowl and make a well in the centre. Slowly pour in 100ml/3½fl oz/generous ⅓ cup cold water and combine with the flour to form a soft dough. Turn the dough out onto a lightly floured surface and knead for 10 minutes until it is smooth and elastic. Shape the dough into a ball, transfer to a lightly oiled bowl, cover with a damp dish towel and leave to rest for 1 hour.

4 Turn the dough out onto a lightly floured surface, roll it into a cylinder and divide into 4–5 equal portions. Take a portion of the dough and roll flat until it is about 2–3mm/¹⁄₁₆in–⅛in thick, then, using a 9cm/3½in cookie cutter, cut out neat circles. Dust the surface of the wrappers lightly with flour so they don't stick together, then stack them on a lightly floured plate. Repeat with the remaining dough portions. Keep any dough you are not using covered with a damp dish towel to prevent it from drying out.

5 Have a small bowl of water by the side to use for sealing the dumplings. Place a gyoza wrapper on the forefront of your hand, then put a heaped tablespoon of the pork filling in the centre. Shape the filling into an oblong shape and flatten it slightly. Wet around the edge of the wrapper with water and bring one side of the wrapper over the filling to form a half-moon shape.

6 Press one corner of the wrapper together to seal, then pinch the edge of the top half of the wrapper next to the seal into a pleat, pushing the pleat into the edge of the bottom half of the wrapper to seal. Continue to work around the edge to the other corner. There should be 6–8 pleats and the bottom half of the wrapper should remain flat.

7 When you've finished pleating the pastry, press gently into the back of the pastry to form a crescent shape. Transfer the gyoza to a lightly floured plate and cover with a damp dish towel while you make the remaining dumplings.

8 Heat the sunflower oil in a large frying pan over a medium-high heat, then arrange the gyoza in the pan. Leave a bit of space between each dumpling to avoid the gyoza sticking together. Cook for 3–4 minutes, then pour in enough hot water to half cover the gyoza. Cover and cook over a medium heat until the liquid has evaporated.

9 Remove the lid and cook for a further 4–5 minutes, or until the bottom of the gyoza becomes brown and crisp. Depending on the size of the frying pan, you may need to cook the gyoza in batches. Serve immediately with shoyu and chilli oil, if you like.

PAK CHOI KIMCHI

MAKES about 700g/1lb 9oz
PREPARATION TIME 30 minutes, plus 4–5 hours resting time and 2 days pickling

1kg/2lb 4oz pak choi/bok choy, roughly chopped into 3cm/1¼in pieces
100g/3½oz/½ cup sea salt
3cm/1¼in piece of fresh ginger, peeled and roughly chopped
6 garlic cloves, roughly chopped
1 onion, roughly chopped
½ red apple, peeled and roughly chopped
30g/1oz Korean red pepper powder or cayenne pepper
2 tbsp granulated sugar
4 spring onions/scallions, chopped

Kimchi is one of the most well-known side dishes in Korean cuisine, and is served at almost every meal. There are many varieties of kimchi, and how they are made varies from region to region and by season. Varieties from the north tend to be a little less spicy than those from the south, where a lot more Korean red pepper powder is used. While cabbage kimchi is the most common kimchi, other vegetables such as pak choi and cucumber are also often used.

1 Put the pak choi in a colander and rinse under running cold water, drain well and transfer to a large bowl or saucepan. Mix the salt together with 500ml/17fl oz/2 cups water until dissolved, then pour the briny liquid over the pak choi. Using both your hands, mix the pak choi and water together, making sure it is well coated with the brine, then leave to stand for 4–5 hours at room temperature.

2 Rinse the pak choi 2–3 times under running cold water to get rid of the brine, then squeeze out the excess liquid and put in a large bowl. Put the ginger, garlic, onion and apple in a food processor or blender and blend until smooth. Transfer the paste to a small bowl and mix in the Korean red pepper powder and sugar. Pour the mixture over the pak choi and tip in the spring onions.

3 Wearing kitchen gloves, thoroughly mix everything together, then transfer the seasoned pak choi to a sterilized preserve jar and seal with a tight-fitting lid. Let the kimchi ferment for 24–48 hours in a cool, dark place before putting in the refrigerator, where it will keep for up to 1 month. Serve cold.

Green tea & black sesame ice cream

SERVES 4
PREPARATION TIME 15 minutes, plus minimum 5–6 hours cooling and freezing time
COOKING TIME 15 minutes

2 tbsp black sesame seeds
500ml/17fl oz/2 cups semi-skimmed/half-fat milk
100ml/3½fl oz/generous ⅓ cup double/heavy cream
2 egg yolks
120g/4¼oz/heaped ½ cup caster/granulated sugar
2 tsp green tea powder

Green tea is a wonderfully versatile ingredient that, apart from making a refreshing hot drink, is an excellent food colouring for natural savoury dishes, cakes and desserts. A bright green ice cream is always a welcome sight on any hot summer day, but with the subtle earthy flavour that comes from the inclusion of toasted ground black sesame, this ice cream is delicious eaten anytime of the year.

1 Heat a frying pan over a medium-high heat, then add the sesame seeds and dry-fry for a few minutes until the seeds begin to pop. Remove from the pan and put in a mini food processor, or use a mortar and pestle, and grind to a coarse powder.

2 Pour the milk and double cream into a saucepan, place over a medium heat and bring just to the boil. Remove from the heat.

3 Meanwhile, using an electric mixer, beat the egg yolks, sugar and green tea powder until light and creamy. With the motor still running, slowly pour in the milk mixture until light and fluffy.

4 Pour the mixture into a clean saucepan over a low heat and cook, stirring continuously, for 10 minutes until it forms a thick custard. Be careful not to overheat or the custard may curdle. Remove from the heat and pour through a fine sieve into a clean bowl. Stir in the ground black sesame seed powder.

5 Leave the custard to cool completely and then pour it into an ice-cream machine. Churn until thick and frozen, according to the manufacturer's instructions, and then transfer to a plastic or metal container, cover and freeze for up to 2 weeks.

mochi ice cream

Great for hot summer days! The chewy texture of the mochi gives a nice contrast to the soft creamy ice cream. For me, it's an East meets West combination that everyone will love.

MAKES **12**
PREPARATION TIME **25 minutes, plus 3–4 hours freezing time**
COOKING TIME **5 minutes**

850g/1lb 14oz Green Tea & Black Sesame Ice Cream (*see previous page*) or ice cream of your choice
100g/3½oz/generous ¾ cup glutinous rice flour
50g/1¾oz/¼ cup caster/granulated sugar
60g/2¼oz/generous ½ cup cornflour/cornstarch, plus extra for dusting

1 Leave the ice cream at room temperature for a few minutes to soften. Line a 12-hole cupcake pan with muffin cases/liners. Use a small scoop to scoop the ice cream into the lined cupcake holes, then immediately put in the freezer for at least 1 hour, or until the ice cream balls are frozen solid.

2 Meanwhile, prepare the mochi dough by adding the glutinous rice flour, 185ml/6fl oz/¾ cup of water and the sugar to a microwave-safe bowl and mixing until well combined.

3 Cover with cling film/plastic wrap and microwave on high (full power) for 1 minute. Using a wet rubber spatula, stir the mixture, then re-cover and microwave on high for another minute. Stir again, re-cover and microwave on high for a further 30 seconds, or until the dough becomes translucent.

4 Dust a clean work surface with some cornflour, place the dough ball on it and press into a flat disc. Sprinkle some more cornflour on top of the dough. Dust some cornflour on the rolling pin and roll the dough to 5mm/¼in thickness.

5 Once the rolled dough is completely cool, cut it into neat discs using an 8cm/3¼in cookie cutter, then place the wrappers on a lightly floured, large baking sheet and cover with a clean dish towel, while you re-roll the dough trimmings and cut out the remaining wrappers to make 12 in total.

6 To assemble, place a wrapper in the palm of your hand, take a frozen ice cream ball and place it in the centre of the wrapper. Fold the lower edge of the wrapper over the ice cream and pinch to seal, gather up the edges to cover the ice cream completely, then pinch and shape into a ball. Wrap it in cling film/plastic wrap to form a nice round ball and place on a clean tray, seam-side down, then transfer to the freezer immediately. Repeat with the remaining wrappers and ice cream balls.

7 Freeze the mochi for at least 2 hours, or until frozen solid. Remove from the freezer and leave to stand at room temperature for about 5 minutes before serving.

CHINA

Chinese cuisine is made up of dishes from the many different regions in China, each varying in taste and appearance. But what is common to all the wonderful dishes that make up Chinese cuisine is the balance of flavours, textures and colours, which are considered to be as important as eating a meal that has a balance of 'Yin' and 'Yang' ingredients. 'Yin' foods, such as Chinese Roast Duck Pancake Rolls (*see pages 54–55*) and the soupy dish, Chinese BBQ Pork Noodle Soup (*see page 57*), are thought to have a cooling effect on the body, whereas 'Yang' foods, such as Beef & Asparagus Stir-Fry (*see page 64*) and Chicken & Sticky Rice in Lotus Leaves (*see page 71*) have warming properties. Rice is one of the staple foods of Chinese cooking. It is always steamed and is served at every meal. Noodles are almost as indispensable as rice, and are normally stir-fried or served in a hot broth.

Key ingredients vary from region to region, but something that is used frequently, everywhere, is fresh ginger, a pungent and spicy root. It lifts the flavour of simple dishes, such as Cantonese Steamed Fish (*see page 66*) and gives depth to other dishes such as Sichuan Mapo Tofu (*see page 60*). Soy sauce is possibly the most important ingredient in Chinese cooking, followed closely by Chinese rice wine. Sesame, Rice Wine & Soy Chicken (*see page 52*) is one very tasty example of a dish that makes good use of both.

sesame, rice wine & soy chicken

SERVES 4
PREPARATION TIME 15 minutes
COOKING TIME 25–30 minutes

600g/1lb 5oz boneless,
  skinless chicken thighs,
  cut into bite-size pieces
1 tsp sunflower oil
1cm/½in piece of fresh
  ginger, peeled and cut into
  fine matchsticks
4 garlic cloves, whole and
  slightly crushed
2 spring onions/scallions, cut
  into 5cm/2in pieces
  lengthways
2 dried chillies, deseeded and
  roughly chopped
125ml/4fl oz/½ cup Shaoxing
  rice wine
3 tbsp light soy sauce
2 tbsp granulated sugar
2 tbsp sesame oil
1 handful of basil leaves
1 handful of coriander/
  cilantro leaves

TO SERVE
1 recipe quantity Boiled
  Long-Grain Rice (*see page
  237*)

This dish originates from the Jiangxi province in southern China, but has become a popular, classic Taiwanese dish. Traditionally, San Bei Ji uses a cup each of sesame oil, rice wine and soy sauce and is simmered in a claypot over a high heat until all the sauce is absorbed by the chicken. I've used a lot less of each to make it less oily and salty.

1 Bring a saucepan of water to the boil and poach the chicken pieces for about 1 minute to seal. Drain and leave to one side.
2 Heat the sunflower oil in a frying pan over a high heat until the oil shimmers and starts to smoke. Add the ginger and stir-fry for 1 minute, then add the garlic and stir-fry for a further 1 minute. Stir in the spring onions and dried chillies and stir-fry for 1 minute. Tip in the chicken, rice wine, soy sauce and sugar, cover the pan and cook for 20–25 minutes until the liquid is evaporated and the chicken is cooked through, stirring occasionally.
3 Meanwhile, heat a claypot or a small heatproof casserole dish over a high heat until very hot. Transfer the chicken pieces from the pan into the claypot, add the sesame oil, basil and coriander and then cover with the lid. Let the chicken sizzle for a few seconds, then serve immediately with boiled rice.

CHINESE ROAST DUCK PANCAKE ROLLS

SERVES 4–6
PREPARATION TIME 25 minutes,
    plus 3–7 hours marinating
    and resting time
COOKING TIME about 1 hour

1 x 1.8kg/4lb whole duck
1 tbsp sea salt
½ tsp Ground Toasted
    Sichuan Pepper (*see page*
    235)
2 tbsp granulated sugar
1 tbsp Shaoxing rice wine
2 star anise
5cm/2in cinnamon stick
3 spring onions/scallions,
    halved
3cm/1¼in piece of fresh
    ginger, peeled and sliced

PANCAKES
250g/9oz/2 cups plain/
    all-purpose flour, plus extra
    for dusting
¼ tsp sea salt
sunflower oil, for oiling
1 tbsp sesame oil

GLAZE
1 tbsp golden syrup or honey
1 tbsp granulated sugar
1 tbsp light soy sauce
1 tbsp rice wine vinegar
¼ tsp five-spice powder

TO SERVE
6 spring onions/scallions, cut
    into fine matchsticks
½ cucumber, halved
    lengthways, deseeded and
    cut into strips
hoisin sauce or plum sauce

This is an all-time favourite of mine that never disappoints – tender duck coated with a flavoursome, glistening, soy sauce and golden syrup glaze, served in steamed pancakes. The most important part of the cooking process is resting the duck in an airy place to dehydrate the skin. This drying process results in a delicate, crispy skin when the duck is cooked.

1 Rinse the duck thoroughly inside and out under running cold water and pat dry inside and out with paper towels. Lightly prick the skin all over with a fork. Rub the salt, Sichuan pepper, sugar and rice wine onto the skin and put the star anise, cinnamon stick, spring onions and ginger in the cavity. Secure the cavity closed with a metal skewer, then transfer the duck to a platter, cover with cling film/plastic wrap and leave to marinate in the refrigerator for about 30 minutes.

2 Bring a large saucepan of water to the boil, then slowly lower in the duck so it is completely submerged. Boil for 5 minutes. Remove the pan from the heat and drain the duck into a colander. Discard the ingredients in the cavity, sit the duck on a wire cooling rack and leave in a well-ventilated area for 5–6 hours, or until all the moisture has evaporated. Alternatively, put in the refrigerator for 2–3 hours.

3 Meanwhile, to prepare the pancakes, mix the flour and salt together in a large bowl. Gradually pour in 185ml/6fl oz/¾ cup hot water and mix with a wooden spoon until it forms a soft, smooth dough. Add a few extra splashes of cold water if the dough is dry. Turn the dough out onto a lightly floured surface and knead for 10–15 minutes until very smooth, then put in a lightly oiled bowl and cover with a damp dish towel or cling film/plastic wrap. Leave to one side for 30 minutes.

4 Pour the sesame oil into a shallow dish. Turn the dough out onto a lightly floured surface, roll it into a cylinder and divide into 8–10 portions of about 30g/1oz each. Take a piece of dough and shape into a ball. Dip the dough in the sesame oil, turning until coated all

round, then place the ball on a clean surface and press into a flat disc. Using a rolling pin, roll into an 18cm/7in disc about 2mm/¹⁄₁₆in thick. Place the disc on a lightly floured surface and repeat with the remaining dough portions.

5 Preheat the oven to 200°C/400°F/Gas 6. To prepare the glaze, mix all the ingredients in a small bowl. Line a baking pan with a sheet of foil, place an oven rack on top and transfer the duck onto the rack. Using a pastry brush, brush the glaze mixture all over the duck.

6 Turn the duck so the breast is facing down. Position the pan on the second lowest shelf in the oven and cook the duck for 15 minutes. After 15 minutes, turn the duck breast-side up. Lower the temperature to 180°C/350°F/Gas 4 and continue to cook the duck for a further 1 hour, or until cooked. After about 45 minutes, brush the glaze mixture all over the duck again. When the tip of a sharp knife is inserted into the thickest part of the meat the juices should run clear. Remove the duck from the oven, pour out any fat or juices from the cavity and leave to one side.

7 Meanwhile, heat a frying pan over a high heat until hot, then reduce the heat to low and cook a pancake for 1–2 minutes on each side until it blisters and light brown spots start to form. Leave to one side, cover with a damp dish towel and cook the remaining pancakes.

8 Steam the pancakes in a bamboo or electric steamer for 5–7 minutes until cooked through just before the duck is ready.

9 Carve the duck meat into slices, removing the skin if it is too fatty, and put on a serving plate with the spring onions, cucumber and hoisin sauce for the pancake rolls to be assembled at the table.

CHINESE BBQ PORK NOODLE SOUP

SERVES 4–6
PREPARATION TIME 25 minutes,
  plus minimum 6 hours
  marinating time and
  making the stock
COOKING TIME 50 minutes,
  plus cooking the noodles

800g/1lb 12oz deboned pork
  shoulder, skin and excess
  fat removed
4 tbsp light soy sauce
1 tbsp oyster sauce
2 tbsp granulated sugar
3 tbsp golden syrup or honey
1 tbsp Shaoxing rice wine
3cm/1¼in piece of fresh
  ginger, peeled, lightly
  crushed and sliced
200g/7oz tenderstem
  broccoli, trimmed
600g/1lb 5oz cooked fresh
  fine egg noodles or
  350g/12oz dried fine egg
  noodles (*see page 238*)
1 recipe quantity Chicken
  Stock (*see page 232*)
2 spring onions/scallions,
  sliced
freshly ground black pepper

BBQ pork, known as Char Siu is one of the most popular Guangdong dishes and goes well with rice or noodles. It can also be used as the filling for Chicken & Vegetable Steamed Buns (*see pages 72–73*). For a really tasty dish, marinate the pork well in advance so that the flavours penetrate the meat.

1 Put the pork in a deep dish or bowl. In a separate bowl, mix together the light soy sauce, oyster sauce, sugar, 2 tablespoons of the golden syrup, rice wine and ginger and season with pepper. Pour the mixture over the pork and then, using your hands, rub the marinade into the pork until it is well coated. Cover with cling film/plastic wrap and leave to marinate in the refrigerator for 6 hours or, for an even better flavour, overnight.

2 Preheat the oven to 180°C/350°F/Gas 4. Remove the pork from the refrigerator and strain off the marinade, keeping the liquid and discarding the solids. Stir the remaining golden syrup into the marinade. Line a baking pan with foil, place an oven rack on top and transfer the pork onto the rack. Place the pan on the second lowest shelf in the oven and cook the pork for 25 minutes. Using tongs, turn over the pork and cook for a further 25 minutes, or until cooked. When the tip of a sharp knife is inserted into the thickest part of the meat, the juices should run clear. Five minutes before the end of cooking, generously brush the marinade all over the pork. Remove the pork from the oven and keep warm.

3 Bring a saucepan of water to the boil and blanch the tenderstem broccoli for 2–3 minutes until tender. Meanwhile, divide the warm, cooked noodles into deep serving bowls. Divide the blanched broccoli into the bowls of noodles.

4 Pour the chicken stock into a saucepan and bring to a gentle boil over a medium heat. Meanwhile, transfer the pork to a chopping/cutting board and cut against the grain into 5mm/¼in slices. Divide the pork into the soup bowls and sprinkle over the spring onions. Ladle the piping hot stock over the noodles and serve immediately.

DAN DAN NOODLES

Egg noodles, topped with pork, drizzled with a vinegary sauce and with a hint of spice from chilli oil. A famous dish from Chengdu, vendors used to transport their noodles in baskets hanging from a bamboo pole carried on their shoulders. 'Dan' is the Chinese word for bamboo pole, giving the dish the name Dan Dan Noodles.

SERVES 4–6
PREPARATION TIME 15 minutes,
  plus 25 minutes soaking
  time
COOKING TIME 20–25 minutes,
  plus cooking the noodles

2 tbsp sunflower oil
1 garlic clove, peeled and
  finely chopped
1cm/½in piece of fresh
  ginger, peeled and finely
  chopped
20g/¾oz dried mushrooms,
  such as shiitake, porcini or
  Chinese mushrooms,
  soaked, drained and
  roughly chopped (*see page
  242*)
350g/12oz minced/ground
  pork
2 tsp light soy sauce
1 tbsp sesame oil
1 tbsp Shaoxing rice wine
1 tbsp finely diced carrot
1 tbsp finely sliced green
  beans
600g/1lb 5oz cooked fresh
  fine egg noodles or
  350g/12oz dried fine egg
  noodles (*see page 238*)
2 spring onions/scallions,
  finely chopped, to serve
freshly ground black pepper

SAUCE
5 tbsp light soy sauce
2 tbsp dark soy sauce
2 tbsp balsamic vinegar

TO SERVE
Chilli Oil (*see page 234 –
  optional*)

1 To make the sauce, mix together the light and dark soy sauces and vinegar with 4 tablespoons warm water in a small bowl. Leave to one side.

2 Heat 1 tablespoon of the sunflower oil in a frying pan over a medium-high heat. Add the garlic and ginger and fry until they start to turn light golden brown, then add the mushrooms and cook for 1 minute.

3 Add the pork, breaking up the lumps. Cook, stirring occasionally, for 5–10 minutes until browned and cooked through, then stir in the soy sauce and sesame oil. Add the rice wine and 3 tablespoons water and simmer for a further 3 minutes. Season with pepper, then leave to one side and keep warm.

4 Meanwhile, heat the remaining 1 tablespoon of oil in a frying pan over a medium heat and stir-fry the carrot and green beans for 1–2 minutes.

5 Divide the cooked noodles into deep soup bowls, then drizzle the sauce mixture over the noodles. Add the pork mixture, carrots and green beans to the bowls, then sprinkle over the spring onions. For a bit of spiciness, add 2–3 teaspoons of the chilli oil, including the chilli flakes, if you like. Serve immediately.

SWEET & SPICY PORK BELLY

SERVES **4–6**
PREPARATION TIME **15 minutes**
COOKING TIME **about 1 hour**

800g/1lb 12oz pork belly,
  cut into bite-size pieces
1 tbsp sunflower oil
1 star anise
5cm/2in cinnamon stick
2 dried chillies, deseeded and
  roughly chopped
3 garlic cloves, finely
  chopped
¼ tsp Sichuan peppercorns
2 tbsp clear honey
2 tbsp light soy sauce
1 tbsp dark soy sauce
1 tbsp Shaoxing rice wine
2 spring onions/scallions, cut
  into 6cm/2½in lengths
2cm/¾in piece of fresh
  ginger, peeled and sliced

TO SERVE
1 recipe quantity Boiled
  Long-Grain Rice (*see page
  237*)

This is a popular dish, regularly cooked in many Chinese households. The method of cooking, however, varies by region. In southern China, the use of dark soy sauce is favoured as it is said it enhances the colour of the dish, whereas in northern China, the colour of the dish is enhanced by the use of sugar, which gives a glossy and caramelized look. A good-quality piece of pork belly is essential to getting the melt-in-your-mouth result that comes from braising the meat in the aromatic sauce.

1 Bring a saucepan of water to the boil, then lower in the pork belly and poach for 3 minutes to seal. Drain and leave to one side.

2 Heat the oil in a saucepan over a medium-high heat. Add the star anise, cinnamon stick and dried chillies and stir-fry for 2–3 minutes until fragrant. Add the garlic and stir-fry for 1–2 minutes, then add the Sichuan peppercorns and stir-fry for 1 minute, or until fragrant.

3 Add the poached pork belly and mix well, then add the honey, light and dark soy sauces, rice wine, spring onions and ginger. Cook for 5 minutes, stirring occasionally, then add 150ml/5fl oz/scant ⅔ cup water. Bring to the boil and cook for a few seconds.

4 Reduce the heat to low and simmer, covered, for 45 minutes, or until the liquid has reduced and thickened and the pork is tender. Serve hot with boiled rice.

SICHUAN MAPO TOFU

This is a famous Sichuan dish that comes with a story. It is said that during the Qing dynasty, a restaurant on the outskirts of Chengdu was well known for a delicious, very spicy tofu dish, which was made by the restaurateur's wife. She had pockmarks on her face, and as a result was called Mapo – *ma* means 'pockmark' and *po* means 'elderly woman', and her signature dish was called Mapo Dou Fu.

SERVES **4**
PREPARATION TIME **10 minutes**
COOKING TIME **20 minutes**

300g/10½oz soft silken tofu, cut into bite-size cubes
1 tbsp sunflower oil
1cm/½in piece of fresh ginger, peeled and finely chopped
3 garlic cloves, finely chopped
200g/7oz minced/ground beef or pork
2 tbsp chilli bean paste
1 tbsp light soy sauce
1 tsp granulated sugar
1 tsp Ground Toasted Sichuan Pepper (*see page 235*)
1 tsp cornflour/cornstarch
2 spring onions/scallions, roughly chopped

TO SERVE
400g/14oz cooked egg noodles (*see page 238*)

1 Bring a large saucepan of water to the boil, then remove from the heat. Carefully tip the tofu into the water and leave to one side.

2 Heat the oil in a wok or frying pan over a medium-high heat. Add the ginger and garlic and stir-fry for 1–2 minutes until fragrant but not coloured. Add the beef or pork, break up the lumps and cook, stirring occasionally, for 5 minutes, or until starting to brown. Add the chilli bean paste, soy sauce, sugar, ground Sichuan pepper and 200ml/7fl oz/scant 1 cup water, then stir to combine and slowly bring to the boil.

3 Carefully drain the tofu and add it to the wok. Gently push the ingredients around the wok until the tofu pieces are coated with the sauce. Do not stir as it may break up the delicate tofu. Let it simmer for 3–5 minutes until heated through.

4 Meanwhile, combine the cornflour with 1 tablespoon water in a small bowl. Slowly pour the cornflour mixture into the wok or pan and gently fold through. Sprinkle over the spring onions and serve immediately with noodles.

SIZZLING BEEF WITH GINGER & SPRING ONIONS

When I was little, as a Friday evening treat, my parents would often take my sister, brother and me out for dinner. There was a particular restaurant we loved that served lip-smacking frog legs on a cast iron sizzle pan, and it is that mouth-watering dish that is the inspiration behind this sizzling beef recipe.

SERVES 4
PREPARATION TIME 10 minutes, plus 40 minutes freezing and marinating time
COOKING TIME 15 minutes

500g/1lb 2oz sirloin, wrapped and semi-frozen for 25 minutes (*see page 242*)
2 tsp cornflour/cornstarch
2 tbsp sunflower oil
2cm/¾in piece of fresh ginger, peeled and cut into thin matchsticks
2 garlic cloves, finely chopped
2 tbsp Shaoxing rice wine
2 tbsp oyster sauce
3 spring onions/scallions, cut lengthways into 6cm/2½in pieces
freshly ground black pepper

TO SERVE
1 recipe quantity Boiled Long-Grain Rice (*see page 237*)

1 Remove the partially frozen beef from the freezer and unwrap the cling film/plastic wrap. Using a sharp knife, cut the beef against the grain into 5mm/¼in slices. Put the beef in a large bowl with the cornflour and toss together until the beef is well coated. Leave to one side for 15 minutes.

2 Heat 1 tablespoon of the oil in a wok or large frying pan over a high heat until smoking hot. Tip in half the marinated beef and stir-fry for 1 minute, or until sealed all round. Remove the beef from the pan, using a slotted spoon, and drain on paper towels. Make sure the wok is still smoking hot, then repeat with the remaining beef.

3 Heat the remaining tablespoon of oil in a clean wok or large frying pan over a medium-high heat. Add the ginger and garlic and stir-fry for 1–2 minutes until fragrant but not coloured. Add the cooked beef slices and toss the ingredients for a few seconds so everything is combined, then add the rice wine and oyster sauce and season with pepper. Cook for 1–2 minutes, tossing occasionally to ensure the ingredients are well combined.

4 Meanwhile, heat a ridged griddle pan, either on the hob/stovetop or by placing it in a very hot oven for about 5 minutes, until it is smoking hot. If you don't have a ridged griddle pan, use a heatproof dish. Add the spring onions and cook, turning occasionally, for 1–2 minutes until golden brown all over.

5 Pour 60ml/2fl oz/¼ cup water into the wok or pan with the beef. Toss the ingredients so everything is well combined, then bring to a gentle boil for a few seconds and toss again. Transfer the beef stir-fry to the griddle pan and let sizzle for a few seconds. Serve immediately with boiled rice.

BeeF & ASPARAGUS StIR-FRY

The wok is an essential piece of equipment in every Chinese kitchen. Its curvy shape means it is hottest at the bottom and enables the heat to rise evenly up the sides. To give your stir-fries some *wok hei* – which simply means the flavour and aroma imparted by the wok – the wok should be intensely hot before you add the ingredients.

SERVES 4–6
PREPARATION TIME **15 minutes,**
   plus 55 minutes freezing
   and marinating time
COOKING TIME **10 minutes**

500g/1lb 2oz beef fillet,
   wrapped and semi-frozen
   for 25 minutes (*see page
   242*)
3 tsp cornflour/cornstarch
3 tbsp light soy sauce
1 tbsp dark soy sauce
1 tbsp oyster sauce
1 tbsp sesame oil
2 tbsp Shaoxing rice wine
1 tsp clear honey
2 tbsp sunflower oil
200g/7oz asparagus, cut
   into bite-size pieces
¼ tsp freshly ground black
   pepper
1cm/½in piece of fresh
   ginger, peeled and finely
   chopped
2 garlic cloves, finely
   chopped
sea salt

TO SERVE
1 recipe quantity Boiled
   Long-Grain Rice (*see
   page 237*)

1 Remove the partially frozen beef from the freezer and unwrap the cling film/plastic wrap. Using a sharp knife, cut the beef against the grain into 5mm/¼in slices.

2 Put the beef in a large bowl with 2 teaspoons of the cornflour, 1 tablespoon of the light soy sauce, the dark soy sauce, oyster sauce, sesame oil, rice wine and honey and toss until the beef is well coated in the marinade. Cover with cling film/plastic wrap and leave to marinate in the refrigerator for 30 minutes.

3 Heat 1 tablespoon of the sunflower oil in a wok over a high heat until smoking hot. Tip in half the marinated beef and stir-fry for 1 minute, or until sealed all round. Remove the beef from the pan, using a slotted spoon, and drain on paper towels. Make sure the wok is still smoking hot, then repeat with the remaining beef.

4 Meanwhile, prepare a large bowl of ice-cold water. Bring a saucepan of water to the boil, add a pinch of salt, tip in the asparagus and cook for 2 minutes, or until al dente. Drain the asparagus and plunge it into the iced water to stop the cooking process.

5 Mix the remaining 2 tablespoons light soy sauce and the pepper with 2 tablespoons water in a small bowl. In another bowl, mix the remaining teaspoon of the cornflour, then slowly pour into the soy sauce mixture, stirring continuously.

6 Heat the remaining tablespoon of oil in a clean wok or large frying pan over a medium-high heat. Add the ginger and garlic and stir-fry for 1–2 minutes until fragrant but not coloured. Drain the asparagus, add to the wok and stir-fry for 1 minute. Add the beef and stir-fry for 2 minutes, then add the cornflour mixture. Toss the ingredients so everything is well combined, then bring to a gentle boil for a few seconds. Serve immediately with boiled rice.

LAMB, COURGETTE & ORANGE STIR-FRY

SERVES 4–6
PREPARATION TIME **15 minutes,**
  plus 25 minutes freezing
  time
COOKING TIME **10 minutes**

500g/1lb 2oz lamb fillet,
  wrapped and semi-frozen
  for 25 minutes (*see
  page 242*)
2 tsp cornflour/cornstarch
1 tbsp oyster sauce
2 tbsp light soy sauce
1 tbsp dark soy sauce
1 tsp granulated sugar
1 tbsp sunflower oil
1 garlic clove, finely chopped
2–3 spring onions/scallions,
  cut into 5cm/2in lengths
1 red chilli, deseeded and
  thinly sliced
1 courgette/zucchini, sliced
½ orange, peeled and cut
  into bite-size pieces
150ml/5fl oz/scant ⅔ cup
  orange juice

TO SERVE
1 recipe quantity Boiled
  Long-Grain Rice (*see
  page 237*)

This dish is light and, with the use of orange and its juice, is fresh-tasting with a touch of citrus sweetness. Traditionally, lamb stir-fries are served with broccoli or asparagus, but here I give it a modern make-over, using courgette instead. The secret to making a delicious stir-fry in minutes is to slice the lamb thinly. It takes less time to cook and the succulent texture is preserved.

1 Remove the partially frozen lamb fillet from the freezer and unwrap the cling film/plastic wrap. Using a sharp knife, cut the lamb against the grain into 5mm/¼in slices. Put the lamb in a bowl with the cornflour, oyster sauce, light and dark soy sauces and sugar and toss until the pieces of lamb are well coated in the sauce. Leave to one side.

2 Heat half of the oil in a wok or large frying pan over a high heat until smoking hot. Tip in the lamb and any liquid and stir-fry for 2 minutes, or until sealed all round. Remove the lamb from the pan, using a slotted spoon, and leave to one side.

3 Heat the remaining oil in the wok or pan over a medium heat, then add the garlic, spring onions and chilli and stir-fry for 1–2 minutes until softened but brown. Add the courgette and stir-fry for about 1 minute, then return the lamb to the wok or pan and stir-fry for a further 2 minutes. Add the orange pieces and juice and bring to a gentle boil for a few seconds. Serve immediately with boiled rice.

cantonese steamed fish

Steaming is one of the most important techniques used in Chinese cooking, and is a very healthy way to cook that retains the flavours of the food, too. A bamboo steamer is ideal, but if you want to steam larger items, such as whole fish, then a wok is handy. In China, the whole fish signifies abundance, and steamed whole fish is a must during Chinese New Year, as it symbolizes a wish for abundance in the New Year.

SERVES 4
PREPARATION TIME **20 minutes**, **plus 45 minutes soaking and marinating time**
COOKING TIME **10 minutes**

1 x 800g/1lb 12oz whole red snapper, sea bream, sea bass or any other white-flesh fish, scaled and gutted by your fishmonger
1 tomato, sliced
1 tbsp light soy sauce
1 tbsp oyster sauce
1 tbsp sesame oil
2 tbsp Shaoxing rice wine
30g/1oz dried mushrooms, such as shiitake, porcini or Chinese mushrooms, soaked, drained and thinly sliced (*see page 242*)
1cm/½in piece of fresh ginger, peeled and cut into fine matchsticks
2 spring onions/scallions, cut into matchsticks
freshly ground black pepper

TO SERVE
1 recipe quantity Boiled Long-Grain Rice (*see page 237*)

1 Rinse the fish inside and out under running cold water and pat dry with paper towels. Using a sharp knife, make three diagonal slits on both sides of the fish. Arrange the tomato on the base of a heatproof platter that will fit inside a wok. Lay the fish on top.

2 Mix together the soy sauce, oyster sauce, sesame oil and rice wine in a small bowl and season with pepper. Pour the sauce over the fish and sprinkle over the mushrooms and ginger. Cover with cling film/plastic wrap and leave to marinate in the refrigerator for about 20 minutes.

3 Place several round cookie cutters or a wire cooling rack with legs at least 2.5cm/1in tall inside a wok. Leaving a minimum gap of 1cm/½in below the steamer, add water to the wok and bring to the boil over a medium-high heat. Set the heatproof plate with the fish on the rack and steam, covered, for 10 minutes, or until the flesh separates from the bone easily and looks opaque when a fork is inserted. Keep an eye on the level of the water, adding more boiling water if necessary. Two minutes before the end of cooking, sprinkle over the spring onions. Serve immediately with boiled rice.

SICHUAN BOILED FISH

Sichuan food is bold and full of characteristics, especially if you like spicy food. This dish uses the full potential of chilli and Sichuan peppercorns to infuse the fish and other ingredients, bringing a lot of dimensions to it – soft and almost melt-in-the-mouth white fish, the pungent, spiciness of chilli and the numbness of the peppercorns. Delicious!

SERVES 4
PREPARATION TIME 15 minutes, plus 30 minutes marinating
COOKING TIME 15–20 minutes

500g/1lb 2oz white fish fillet, such as cod, haddock, catfish or flounder
½ tsp sea salt
¼ tsp ground white pepper
1 tbsp sesame oil
1 tbsp Shaoxing rice wine
1 tbsp cornflour/cornstarch
15 dried red chillies, deseeded and roughly chopped
1 tbsp Sichuan peppercorns
1 tbsp, plus 100ml/3½fl oz/ scant ½ cup sunflower oil
1 small carrot, cut into matchsticks
120g/4¼oz/generous 1 cup bean sprouts
2cm/¾in piece of fresh ginger, peeled and cut into thin matchsticks
2 garlic cloves, finely chopped
1 tbsp chilli bean paste
1 tbsp light soy sauce
1 tsp granulated sugar
2 spring onions/scallions, roughly chopped
1 small handful of coriander/ cilantro leaves, roughly chopped

TO SERVE
1 recipe quantity Boiled Long-Grain Rice (*see page 237*)

1 Place the fish fillet horizontally on a chopping/cutting board. Angle the knife at 45° to the fillet and cut the fillet against the grain into slices of about 3cm/1¼in wide and 3–5mm/⅛–¼in thick.

2 Mix the salt, white pepper, sesame oil, rice wine and cornflour in a bowl. Add the fish and thoroughly coat with the marinade. Cover with cling film/plastic wrap. Leave to marinate in the refrigerator for 30 minutes.

3 Heat a wok over a medium-low heat, then add the dried chillies and Sichuan peppercorns and dry-fry for a few minutes, or until fragrant. Remove from the heat and set aside.

4 Heat ½ tablespoon of sunflower oil in the same wok over a medium-high heat. Add the carrot and stir-fry for about 2 minutes. Remove from the pan, transfer to a heatproof serving bowl and set aside. Add the other ½ tablespoon of sunflower oil to the wok, still over a medium-high heat, repeat the same process with the bean sprouts, then layer the bean sprouts on top of the stir-fried carrot.

5 Using the same wok over a medium-high heat, add the ginger and garlic and stir-fry for about 1 minute, or until fragrant. Tip in the chilli bean paste, soy sauce and sugar. Pour in 400ml/ 14fl oz/generous 1½ cups of water and bring to the boil. Add in the fried dried chillies and Sichuan peppercorns, then add the fish and marinade and stir gently to separate each piece. Bring to the boil for 1–2 minutes, then pour everything on top of the stir-fried carrot and bean sprouts. Sprinkle over the spring onions and coriander.

6 Meanwhile, heat the rest of the sunflower oil in a deep, heavy-based saucepan to 170°C/325°F, or until a small piece of bread turns brown in 20 seconds. Pour the heated oil evenly over all the ingredients in the bowl. Serve hot with boiled rice.

macaroni soup with ham & fried egg

SERVES **4**
PREPARATION TIME **15 minutes**,
   plus making the stock
COOKING TIME **20 minutes**

250g/9oz dried macaroni
1 recipe quantity Chicken
   Stock (*see page 232*)
1 tbsp light soy sauce
200g/7oz frozen mixed
   vegetables
1 tbsp sunflower oil
4 eggs
8 slices ham, cut into
   small squares
1 spring onion/scallion,
   finely chopped

This is not your typical pasta dish. It's an Asian dish with a Western twist that brings you comfort day or night, summer or winter.

1 Fill a large saucepan with plenty of water and bring to the boil, then add the macaroni and cook according to the package instructions, or until al dente, then drain and set aside.
2 Meanwhile, bring the chicken stock to the boil in a separate pan and add the soy sauce. Tip in the mixed vegetables, reduce the heat to medium and simmer for a few minutes.
3 Heat the oil in a frying pan over a medium heat and fry the eggs for about 3 minutes each – the yolks should still be runny.
4 To assemble, divide the warm macaroni into individual bowls, then divide the mixed vegetables (using a slotted spoon) and the ham between the bowls. Bring the chicken stock to a vigorous boil. Add the spring onion, then ladle the piping hot stock into the bowls. Top each bowl with a fried egg and serve immediately.

CHICKeN & Sticky RICe
in Lotus Leaves

SERVES **4**
PREPARATION TIME **about 1 hour**
COOKING TIME **50–55 minutes**

1 tsp granulated sugar
2 tbsp light soy sauce
1 tbsp dark soy sauce
1 tbsp oyster sauce
1 tbsp sesame oil
2cm/¾in piece of fresh
   ginger, peeled and finely
   grated, pulp discarded,
   reserving the juice
1 tbsp Shaoxing rice wine
1 tsp cornflour/cornstarch
600g/1lb 5oz boneless,
   skinless chicken thighs,
   cut into bite-size pieces
500g/1lb 2oz/2½ cups
   jasmine rice, soaked
   for 30 minutes
30g/1oz dried shrimps
1 tbsp sunflower oil
120g/4¼oz air-dried sausage,
   such as Chinese sausage or
   chorizo, diced (optional)
30g/1oz dried mushrooms,
   such as shiitake, porcini or
   Chinese mushrooms,
   soaked, drained and roughly
   chopped (*see page 242*)
4 dried lotus leaves (optional)
freshly ground black pepper

RICE SEASONING
¼ tsp sea salt
1 tbsp granulated sugar
1 tbsp light soy sauce
2 tbsp dark soy sauce
1 tbsp oyster sauce
2 tbsp sesame oil

1 Mix the sugar, light and dark soy sauces, oyster sauce, sesame oil, ginger juice, rice wine and cornflour in a large bowl until combined, then season with pepper. Add the chicken and toss until each piece of chicken is well coated with the marinade. Cover with cling film/plastic wrap and leave to marinate in the refrigerator for at least 2 hours.

2 Drain the soaking rice and transfer to a bowl. Mix all the rice seasoning ingredients together and season with black pepper, then mix through the rice until well combined.

3 Place a sheet of greaseproof paper on the base of a bamboo or electric steamer and spread the rice mixture out on top. Sprinkle over 1 tablespoon water, then steam the rice for 30 minutes. After 15 minutes, sprinkle over a further 1–2 tablespoons water. Remove the rice from the steamer and leave to one side to cool.

4 Meanwhile, put the dried shrimps in a small bowl, cover with water and leave to soak for 5–10 minutes. Drain well and set aside.

5 Heat the sunflower oil in a frying pan over a medium-high heat, then add the air-dried sausage, if using, and stir-fry for 1 minute. Add the mushrooms and soaked shrimps and stir-fry for 2 minutes. Tip in the marinated chicken and cook for 5 minutes, or until the chicken starts to turn opaque, stirring occasionally. Add 3 tablespoons water and cook for a further 3–4 minutes, or until the chicken starts to turn golden brown. Transfer to a bowl and leave to one side.

6 Fill a large saucepan or wok with water and bring to the boil. Slowly submerge the lotus leaves into the water and cook for 1–2 minutes until soft. Refresh under running cold water and pat dry with paper towels. Trim off the hard stems and cut the leaves in quarters.

7 To assemble, layer 2 pieces of lotus leaf together and spoon 2 heaped tablespoons of rice in the centre. Fatten the rice, then spread 3 heaped tablespoons of chicken filling evenly over the top. Spoon another heaped tablespoon of rice over the chicken. Fold the bottom of the leaves over the filling, then the sides and roll the parcel to enclose. Continue with the remaining ingredients to make a total of 8 parcels. Steam the parcels in a bamboo or electric steamer for 20–25 minutes until cooked through. Ensure heat is maintained throughout the steaming process. Serve immediately.

CHICKEN & VEGETABLE STEAMED BUNS

MAKES 25 small buns
PREPARATION TIME 2 hours
45 minutes, plus cooling time
COOKING TIME 20–30 minutes

1 tsp sesame oil
1 tbsp light soy sauce
1 tbsp dark soy sauce
1 tbsp oyster sauce
1 tbsp Shaoxing rice wine
2 tsp granulated sugar
½ tsp cornflour/cornstarch
350g/12oz boneless, skinless chicken thighs or chicken breasts, trimmed and cut into bite-size pieces
2 tbsp sunflower oil
2 garlic cloves, finely chopped
1cm/½in piece of fresh ginger, peeled and finely chopped
1 carrot, cut into matchsticks
200g/7oz Jerusalem artichokes, water chestnuts or jicamas, peeled and cut into matchsticks
1 tbsp sesame seeds
2 spring onions/scallions, finely chopped
freshly ground black pepper

BUN DOUGH
70g/2½oz caster/superfine sugar
1 tsp Shaoxing rice wine
10g/¼oz dried active yeast
400g/14oz/3¼ cups plain/all-purpose flour, plus extra for dusting
2 tsp baking powder

I use chicken here, but leftover barbecued or roast pork also works. The buns freeze really well, so if you don't need the full quantity, you can freeze them steamed. All you then need to do for a delicious dim sum in minutes is to thaw the buns before steaming.

1 Combine the sesame oil, light and dark soy sauces, oyster sauce, rice wine, sugar and cornflour in a large bowl, stirring until the sugar is dissolved. Season with pepper, then add the chicken and toss until each piece of chicken is well coated with the marinade. Cover with cling film/plastic wrap and leave to marinate in the refrigerator for at least 2 hours.

2 To make the bun dough, mix together the sugar, rice wine, yeast and 270ml/9½fl oz/generous 1 cup water until the sugar is dissolved. Leave to stand for 10 minutes or until foaming. In a large mixing bowl, combine the flour and baking powder and make a well in the centre. Slowly pour in the sugared liquid and combine with the flour to form a soft dough.

3 Turn the dough out onto a lightly floured surface and knead for 10 minutes until it is smooth and elastic. Shape the dough into a ball, put in a bowl and cover with a damp dish towel. Leave in a warm place for 45 minutes–1 hour until it has doubled in size.

4 Heat 1 tablespoon of the sunflower oil in a frying pan over a medium-high heat. Add the garlic and ginger and cook, stirring occasionally, for 1–2 minutes until fragrant but not coloured. Add the carrot and Jerusalem artichokes and cook for 10 minutes. Add 2 tablespoons water and cook for a further 5–10 minutes until the vegetables have softened. Remove from the heat and leave to cool.

5 Meanwhile, heat a frying pan over a medium heat, then add the sesame seeds and dry-roast until fragrant and starting to brown. Remove and leave to one side. Add the remaining tablespoon of sunflower oil to the pan and heat over a medium-high heat. When hot, add the marinated chicken and cook for 10–15 minutes until golden brown and cooked through. Add the toasted sesame seeds, spring onions and 1 tablespoon water and cook for 1 minute.

Remove from the heat and combine with the carrot and Jerusalem artichoke stir-fry. Leave to one side to cool.

6 Turn the dough out onto a lightly floured surface and divide in half. Roll each piece of dough into a cylinder, then divide the cylinders into 25 equal portions. Shape the dough portions into balls, covering them with a damp dish towel as you go so they don't dry out. Leave the balls to rest for 15 minutes. Meanwhile, cut up 25 small squares of greaseproof paper for the buns to rest on when they are cooked.

7 Lightly dust the work surface with flour again, then take a dough ball and flatten it with the palm of your hand. Using a rolling pin, roll the dough into a 10cm/4in disc. Place the disc on the palm of your hand and put 1 heaped tablespoon of the cooled filling in the centre. Gather up the edge of the dough around the filling to create a small bag shape. Twist and pinch together the gathered pleats of dough to seal, then put the bun on a small square of greaseproof paper, pleat-side up, and cover with a damp dish towel. Repeat to make up the remaining buns, then leave the buns to rest for about 30 minutes.

8 Keeping the greaseproof paper beneath the buns, arrange them in a bamboo or electric steamer. Leave a space equal to half the size of a bun between each one so they don't stick together during cooking. Steam the buns in batches for 5–7 minutes until soft and fluffy to the touch, but not springy. Serve hot.

STEAMED PRAWN DUMPLINGS

MAKES **about 32**
PREPARATION TIME **1 hour
30 minutes, plus 1 hour
marinating time**
COOKING TIME **15–20 minutes**

150g/5½oz raw, peeled large
  king prawns/jumbo shrimp,
  deveined and cut into small
  cubes (*see page 241*)
20g/¾oz bamboo shoots,
  finely chopped
1 tsp cornflour/cornstarch
½ tsp sea salt
½ tsp granulated sugar
½ tsp chicken stock/bouillon
  powder
½ tsp sesame oil
freshly ground black pepper

HAR GOW WRAPPERS
200g/7oz/1⅓ cup wheat
  starch, plus extra for
  dusting
2 tbsp cornflour/cornstarch
¼ tsp fine sea salt
40ml/1¼fl oz vegetable oil,
  plus extra for oiling

TO SERVE
Chilli Oil (*see page 234 –
  optional*)

1 Toss the prawns and bamboo shoots together in a bowl, then add the cornflour and stir in with a wooden spoon. Add the salt, sugar, chicken stock powder and sesame oil and mix until well combined. Season with pepper, cover with cling film/plastic wrap and refrigerate for 1 hour.

2 Meanwhile, to make the har gow wrappers, mix together the wheat starch, cornflour and salt in a bowl. Pour in 125ml/4fl oz/½ cup boiling water and stir with a wooden spoon to form a dough. Cover with a damp dish towel and cool for 20 minutes, then add the vegetable oil and knead until the dough is very smooth.

3 Roll the dough into a long sausage shape on a lightly floured surface, then divide it into 32 equal portions. Shape each portion into a ball and flatten slightly between your palms. Place a dough piece on an oiled surface or chopping/cutting board and, using a rolling pin, roll into a 9cm/3½in disc. Cut the rolled dough into a neat disc using an 8cm/3¼in cookie cutter, then place the wrapper on a large, lightly floured baking sheet, cover with a damp dish towel and make the remaining wrappers.

4 To assemble the dumplings, place a wrapper on the palm of your hand. Spoon 3–4 heaped teaspoons of the filling in the centre of the wrapper and flatten slightly. Fold the lower edge of the wrapper over the filling to form a half-moon shape, leaving a small gap at the top of the lower half of the wrapper.

5 Pinch the pastry along the curve to seal, then working from one corner of the sealed pastry, use your thumb and index finger to fold over and pinch the pastry together to form a pleat. Continue to work around the edge to the top of the curve, then repeat from the other corner. Each side should have 5–6 pleats, and the underneath of the dumpling should remain flat. Press gently into the base of the pastry to form a crescent shape, then place the dumpling on a lightly oiled plate and cover with a damp dish towel. Repeat for the remaining dumplings.

6 Place a sheet of greaseproof paper on the base of a bamboo or electric steamer and lightly oil. Arrange about 8 dumplings on the paper, leaving a gap between each dumpling so they don't stick together, and steam for 3–4 minutes until cooked through. Repeat until all the dumplings are cooked. Serve immediately with chilli oil.

Sweet Peanut & Sesame Balls

MAKES 20–22
PREPARATION TIME 50 minutes
COOKING TIME 20–30 minutes

70g/2½oz/scant ⅓ cup
caster/superfine sugar
320g/11¼oz/heaped 1¾ cups
glutinous rice flour, plus
extra for dusting
100g/3½oz/scant ⅔ cup
skinless raw peanuts
80g/2¾oz/heaped ⅓ cup
granulated sugar
500ml/17fl oz/2 cups
sunflower oil, for
deep-frying
60g/2¼oz/scant ½ cup
sesame seeds

These little gems are generously coated with sesame seeds and have a gorgeous crispy base. The texture of the pastry is slightly chewy and the filling is smooth with crunchy bits from the peanuts. A classic sweet that is still a family favourite.

1 Add the caster sugar to 250ml/9fl oz/1 cup water and stir until dissolved. Put the glutinous rice flour into a large mixing bowl and make a well in the centre. Slowly pour in the sugared water and combine with the flour to form a soft dough. Turn the dough out onto a lightly floured surface, roll it into a cylinder and divide into 20–22 equal portions.

2 Heat a frying pan over a medium-high heat, then add the peanuts and dry-roast until fragrant and starting to brown. Remove from the heat and roughly grind in a food processor or blender – you want a fine powder with some chunky bits. Tip the ground peanuts into a bowl and add the granulated sugar, 2 tablespoons of the oil and 3 tablespoons water. Stir into a rough paste and leave to one side.

3 Fill a small bowl with water and pour the sesame seeds onto a small plate. Take a portion of the dough, shape it into a ball and then press into an 8cm/3¼in disc. Flatten the edges so the centre of the disc is slightly thicker. Spoon 1–2 heaped teaspoons of the peanut paste into the centre of the pastry, gather up the edges and shape into a ball. Repeat for the remaining peanut balls, then dip each ball in the water and coat with the sesame seeds.

4 Heat the remaining oil in a deep, heavy-based saucepan to 170°C/325°F, or until a small piece of bread turns brown in 20 seconds. Gently slide 3–4 sesame balls into the oil and fry for 3–4 minutes until golden brown. Make sure the oil doesn't get too hot so the sesame seeds don't burn and use a slotted spoon to push the balls down into the oil so they cook evenly. Using the slotted spoon, remove the sesame balls from the oil and drain on paper towels. Repeat until all the balls are cooked. Serve hot or cold.

PHILIPPINES
& INDONESIA

Filipino cuisine is an exotic fusion of Chinese and Spanish cuisines with hints of influences from the Americas and other Asian countries. A popular dish, demonstrating the Chinese influence, is Filipino Prawn & Pork Noodles (*see page 88*). A modern twist here is the use of saffron threads instead of the traditional and common colouring ingredient called achiote seeds. South American influences can be seen in the dish Citrus-Cured Tuna & Tomato Salad (*see page 94*), which is similar to ceviche and uses a number of key ingredients in Filipino cooking, such as chilli, coriander, garlic and ginger. Other storecupboard essentials are fish sauce, vinegar, pepper and tamarind. A dish like Beef, Peanut & Vegetable Stew (*see page 84*) is a good example of Spanish influence, where the techniques of boiling and braising are used.

Indonesia, often referred to as the world's largest archipelago with more than 18,000 islands, also has a rich history and this can be seen in its flavoursome cuisine, which can be hot, sweet, sour and salty, but often has fragrant undertones that come from the use of coconut milk and lemongrass. Both the fresh and dried varieties of the spices coriander, turmeric and chilli play an important role in Indonesian cooking, as do cumin and pepper. The very popular Balinese Fish Satay (*see page 97*) is an example of good use of these aromatic spices, which may be used also as a rub, such as in Balinese Roast Duck in Banana Leaves (*see page 83*), or combined in spice pastes and used in stir-fries such as Indonesian Chicken Fried Rice (*see page 80*).

INDONESIAN CHICKEN FRIED RICE

SERVES 4
**PREPARATION TIME 45 minutes,
plus cooking and chilling
the rice**
COOKING TIME 20–25 minutes

1 green bird's eye chilli,
   deseeded and roughly
   chopped
2 red chillies, deseeded and
   roughly chopped
2 shallots, roughly chopped
3 garlic cloves, roughly
   chopped
½ tsp roasted shrimp paste
   (see page 242)
1 tsp grated palm sugar or
   soft light brown sugar
60g/2¼oz dried anchovies
2 tbsp sunflower oil
200g/7oz skinless, boneless
   chicken breast, cut into
   bite-size pieces
80g/2¾oz green beans,
   finely sliced
1 recipe quantity Boiled
   Long-Grain Rice, cooked
   the night before and chilled
   (see page 237)
2 tbsp light soy sauce
2 tbsp dark soy sauce
1 tbsp clear honey
1 small handful of coriander/
   cilantro leaves, finely
   chopped
sea salt

TO SERVE
1 handful of Indonesian
   prawn crackers (krupuk)
Sambal (see page 236)

1 Put the green bird's eye chilli, red chillies, shallots, garlic and shrimp paste in a mortar and pestle or a food processor and blend to a smooth paste. Transfer to a bowl and add a pinch of salt and the sugar. Mix well and leave to one side.

2 Soak the dried anchovies in water for 1–2 minutes, then drain and pat dry with paper towel, squeezing out any excess liquid. Heat 1 tablespoon of the oil in a frying pan over a medium-high heat. Add the anchovies and stir-fry for 1–2 minutes until golden brown. Leave to one side.

3 Heat the remaining tablespoon of oil in a wok or large frying pan over a high heat until smoking hot. Add the chilli paste and stir-fry for 3–4 minutes until fragrant. Tip in the chicken pieces and stir-fry for 5 minutes, or until cooked through and starting to turn golden. Add the green beans and cook for about 3 minutes, or until tender.

4 Add the boiled rice, break up any lumps and stir-fry for 5–10 minutes until the chicken is cooked and the rice is hot. Add the light and dark soy sauces and honey and mix in well. Tip in the fried anchovies and coriander and stir until well combined. Serve immediately with the prawn crackers and sambal on the side.

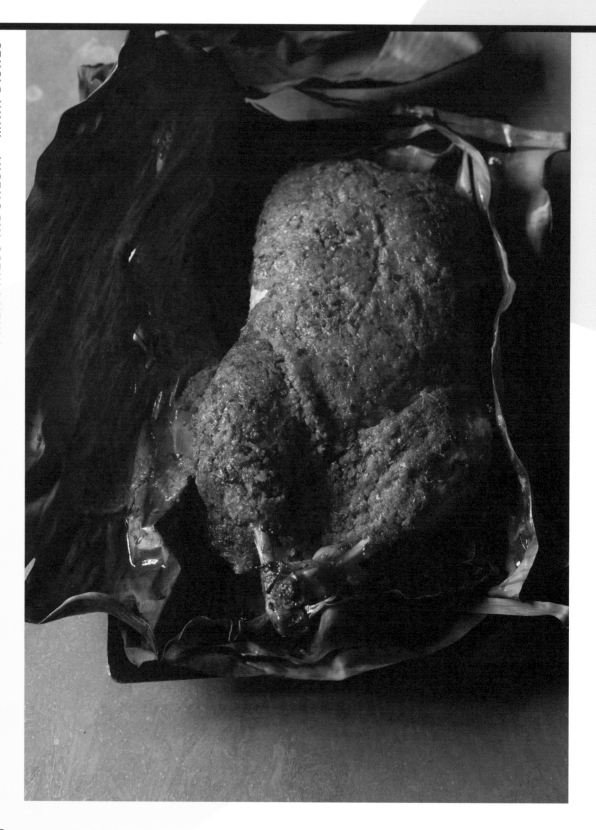

BALINESE ROAST DUCK IN BANANA LEAVES

SERVES 4–6
PREPARATION TIME 20 minutes,
plus minimum 3 hours
marinating time
COOKING TIME 2 hours

1 x 1.8kg/4lb whole duck
enough banana leaves or foil
  for wrapping
1 recipe quantity Boiled
  Long-Grain Rice (*see*
  page 237)

MARINADE
10 shallots, roughly chopped
6 garlic cloves, roughly
  chopped
2 lemongrass stalks, outer leaves
  and stalk ends removed,
  crushed and roughly chopped
4 kaffir lime leaves, roughly
  chopped
4cm/1½in piece of fresh
  ginger, peeled and roughly
  chopped
5 red chillies, deseeded and
  roughly chopped
2 green bird's eye chillies,
  deseeded and roughly
  chopped
2 tsp roasted shrimp paste
  (*see page 242*)
½ tsp black peppercorns
4 macadamia nuts
2cm/¾in piece of fresh turmeric,
  peeled and roughly chopped or
  1 tsp ground turmeric
1 tsp ground coriander
½ tsp ground cumin
1 tsp sea salt
1 tsp clear honey
1 tbsp lime juice

1 Rinse the duck thoroughly inside and out under running cold water and pat dry inside and out with paper towels. Lightly prick the skin all over with a fork.

2 Put all the marinade ingredients in a food processor, except the ground turmeric, if using, coriander, cumin, salt, honey and lime juice and blend to a smooth paste. Transfer to a small bowl and stir in the remaining ingredients. Rub the duck inside and out with the marinade until it is well coated. Layer the banana leaves or foil on a large plate and wrap up the duck. Secure with cocktail sticks, if necessary. Cover with cling film/plastic wrap and leave to marinate in the refrigerator for 3–4 hours or, for an even better flavour, overnight.

3 Preheat the oven to 200°C/400°F/Gas 6. Put the duck on an oven rack over a baking sheet and place on the middle shelf of the oven. Cook for 15 minutes, then reduce the temperature to 180°C/350°F/Gas 4 and continue to cook for 1½–2 hours until cooked. When the tip of a sharp knife is inserted into the thickest part of the meat, the juices should run clear.

4 Unwrap the duck, then using a sharp carving knife, slice the meat into pieces. Serve hot with boiled rice.

Beef, Peanut & Vegetable Stew

Traditionally, this Filipino stew is made with oxtail, a variety of vegetables and a peanut spice paste. I have used chuck steak, cut into bite-size pieces. It is a hearty dish made with inexpensive ingredients and is quick to prepare, but it does need some patience while it simmers away, the meat tenderizes and the flavours develop.

SERVES 6
PREPARATION TIME **15 minutes**
COOKING TIME **about 2 hours 30 minutes**

150g/5½oz/scant 1 cup skinless raw peanuts
1.5–1.8kg/3lb 5oz–4lb casserole steak, trimmed of fat and cut into bite-size pieces
1 tbsp sunflower oil
a large pinch of saffron threads
2 onions, roughly chopped
8 garlic cloves, chopped
1 recipe quantity Kare Kare Spice Paste (*see page 228*)
200g/7oz green beans, trimmed and cut into 6cm/2½in pieces
1 medium aubergine/ eggplant, cut into bite-size pieces
200g/7oz baby carrots, trimmed
2 tbsp lime juice or 1 recipe quantity Tamarind Water (*see page 242*)
sea salt

TO SERVE
1 recipe quantity Boiled Long-Grain Rice (*see page 237*)

1 Heat a frying pan over a medium-high heat, then add the peanuts and dry-roast until fragrant and starting to brown. Remove from the heat and roughly grind the peanuts in a food processor or blender – you want a fine powder with some chunky bits. Leave to one side.

2 Rinse the beef under running cold water and pat dry with paper towels. Heat the oil in a large casserole dish over a medium-high heat, then add half the casserole steak and stir-fry for 4–5 minutes until beginning to brown. Remove the beef from the pan, using a slotted spoon, and drain on paper towels. Repeat with the remaining beef, adding more oil as required.

3 Mix together the saffron and 2 tablespoons warm water in a small bowl and leave to one side. Place the casserole dish back over a medium-high heat, then add the onions and garlic and stir-fry for 2 minutes, or until soft and translucent. Add the spice paste and cook gently, stirring occasionally, for 10–15 minutes until fragrant and the oil starts to rise to the surface, then add the beef pieces and combine well. Add the saffron and the soaking liquid and pour in 270ml/9½fl oz/generous 1 cup water. Bring to the boil, cover with a tight-fitting lid, reduce the heat to low and simmer for about 1 hour, skimming off any scum that rises to the surface from time to time.

4 After 1 hour of cooking, tip the ground peanuts, green beans, aubergine, carrots and lime juice into the stew and season with salt. Give it a good stir to coat the vegetables evenly with the mixture and continue to simmer for at least a further 1 hour, or until the beef is almost falling apart and the sauce has thickened. Serve immediately with boiled rice.

MAKASSAR BEEF SOUP

This soup originates from the island of Sulawesi, Indonesia. It is wonderfully aromatic, with the citrus of the lemongrass and earthiness of spices balancing the richness of the beef perfectly. To make a substantial meal, you can serve it with rice noodles.

SERVES 4–6
PREPARATION TIME 30 minutes, plus 10 minutes cooling time
COOKING TIME about 1 hour

1 x 500g/1lb 2oz beef tenderloin
¼ tsp white peppercorns
1 tbsp granulated sugar
2 lemongrass stalks, outer leaves and stalk ends removed and crushed
1 onion, sliced
2 tsp lime juice
2 tbsp sunflower oil
1 recipe quantity Coto Makassar Spice Paste (*see page 227*)

TO SERVE
400g/14oz cooked rice noodles (*see page 238*)
2 spring onions/scallions, finely chopped
1 small handful of coriander/cilantro leaves, chopped
1 small handful of mint leaves, chopped
2 tbsp Fried Shallots (*see page 235*)

1 Place the beef horizontally on a chopping/cutting board, then use a paring knife or a flexible, fine-bladed knife to trim away fat and silver skin. To trim the silver skin, slip the knife between the meat and the silver skin and slide the knife along the length of the beef. Continue this process until all the silver skin is removed.

2 Put the beef, white peppercorns, sugar, lemongrass, onion and 1.75 litres/60fl oz/7 cups water in a large saucepan over a high heat and bring to the boil. Skim any scum from the surface, then reduce the heat to low and simmer gently for 30 minutes.

3 Remove the beef from the stock and leave for 5–10 minutes to cool. Using a sharp knife, cut the tenderloin into strips about 3mm/⅛in thick. Return the meat pieces to the stock, add the lime juice and continue to simmer for 15–20 minutes.

4 Meanwhile, heat the oil in a large frying pan over a medium-high heat. Add the spice paste and cook gently, stirring occasionally, for 10–15 minutes until fragrant and the oil starts to rise to the surface. Pour in the stock and beef and simmer for 10–15 minutes until the beef is tender. Serve immediately sprinkled with the rice noodles, spring onions, coriander, mint and fried shallots.

PRAWN & TAMARIND SOUP

SERVES 4–6
PREPARATION TIME 15 minutes
COOKING TIME 20 minutes

800g/1lb 12oz raw, unpeeled large king prawns/jumbo shrimp
2 shallots, quartered
2 green bird's eye chillies, whole
100g/3½oz green beans, cut into 5cm/2in pieces
2 tomatoes, skinned and quartered (*see page 242*)
1 recipe quantity Tamarind Water (*see page 242*)
2 tsp granulated sugar
juice of 1 lime
150g/5½oz baby leaf spinach
sea salt

TO SERVE
400g/14oz cooked rice noodles (*see page 238*)

When I first tasted this soup it reminded me of the tanginess and spiciness of Prawn Tom Yum Soup (*see page 151*), which got me thinking how a lot of Southeast Asian food shares many similarities. Traditionally, water spinach is used, but I have substituted baby leaf spinach instead. This is a Filipino soup that is rich in colour and flavour.

1 Using a pair of kitchen scissors, trim from each prawn the feelers, rostrum, legs and the sharp end of the tail. Make a slit along the back of the prawn with a sharp knife and pull out the black vein with the tip of the knife or your fingers. Rinse the prawns under running cold water and pat dry with paper towels.

2 Bring 1.5 litres/52fl oz/6 cups water to the boil in a large saucepan over a medium-high heat. Add the shallots and chillies and cook for 2 minutes, then add the green beans and cook for a further 1–2 minutes. Reduce the heat to low, add the tomatoes and simmer for 2 minutes until the tomatoes begin to soften.

3 Add the prawns and cook, covered, for 4–5 minutes until the prawns turn pink and are cooked through. Add the tamarind water and sugar, then season with salt and add the lime juice, to taste. Bring back to the boil for a few seconds, then add the spinach and cook for 1 minute, or until it starts to wilt. Serve immediately with rice noodles.

FILIPINO PRAWN & PORK NOODLES

SERVES 4–6
PREPARATION TIME 25 minutes
COOKING TIME about
    30 minutes

250g/9oz raw, peeled large
    king prawns/jumbo shrimp,
    heads removed, with tails
    left on and deveined (*see
    page 241*)
2 tbsp sunflower oil
100g/3½oz firm tofu, cut
    into 2cm/¾in cubes
100g/3½oz minced/ground
    pork
2 tsp cornflour/cornstarch
a pinch of saffron threads
3 tbsp fish sauce
1 tsp granulated sugar
200g/7oz rice vermicelli,
    soaked according to packet
    instructions
3 hard-boiled eggs, cut into
    wedges
2 tbsp Fried Shallots
    (*see page 235*)
2 spring onions/scallions,
    sliced into fine strips
    lengthways
80g/2¾oz Toasted Dried
    Anchovies (*see page 242 –
    optional*)
sea salt and freshly ground
    black pepper

TO SERVE
1 lime, cut into wedges

Originally introduced by the Chinese, noodle dishes are a household staple in almost all Filipino homes. In the Chinese culture noodles symbolize longevity, so this dish, which is also a very colourful and festive dish, is a popular choice to serve at birthday celebrations.

1 Pour 250ml/9fl oz/1 cup water into a large saucepan and bring to the boil over a medium-high heat. Tip in the prawns and cook until they turn pink and are cooked through. Using a slotted spoon, remove the prawns and keep warm. Reserve the water.

2 Heat 1 tablespoon of the oil in a frying pan over a medium-high heat. Add the tofu and stir-fry for 2–3 minutes until golden brown and crispy all over. Remove from the pan and leave to one side.

3 Reduce the heat to medium and add the remaining 1 tablespoon of oil to the pan. When the oil is hot, add the pork, breaking up any lumps. Increase the heat to high and cook for 5–10 minutes, stirring frequently. Meanwhile, mix together the cornflour and 1 tablespoon water in a small bowl.

4 Pour the reserved liquid from the prawns into the pan and bring to the boil over a high heat for a few seconds, then reduce the heat to medium-low. Add the saffron, fish sauce and sugar and season with salt and pepper. Stir in the cornflour mixture and bring back to a gentle boil. Reduce the heat to low and simmer for 5 minutes.

5 Meanwhile, bring plenty of water to the boil in a large saucepan. Drain the soaking rice vermicelli and add to the pan. Cook for 2–3 minutes until softened. Drain the noodles well and put on a serving plate.

6 Bring the simmering sauce to the boil for a few seconds and then remove from the heat. Ladle the sauce over the noodles and divide the fried tofu, prawns and hard-boiled eggs into the bowls. Sprinkle over the fried shallots, spring onions and anchovies, if using. Serve immediately with lime wedges.

GADO GADO

The main feature of Gado Gado, a popular Indonesian vegetable salad, is the peanut sauce that transforms all the simple ingredients into a harmonious bowl of flavours. And to give it additional crunch, *krupuk*, Indonesian prawn crackers, are served sprinkled over the top or whole. This salad works well with all sorts of vegetables, so do experiment.

SERVES **4**
PREPARATION TIME **1 hour**
COOKING TIME **about 30 minutes**

150g/5½oz/scant 1 cup skinless raw peanuts
3 tbsp sunflower oil
1 recipe quantity Gado Gado Spice Paste (*see page 227*)
1 tbsp lime juice or ½ recipe quantity Tamarind Water (*see page 242*)
2 tbsp granulated sugar
100g/3½oz firm tofu, sliced
150g/5½oz green beans, trimmed and cut into 6cm/2½in pieces
150g/5½oz/1¼ cups bean sprouts or edamame
1 small cucumber, halved lengthways, deseeded and chunkily sliced
1 small carrot, cut into matchsticks
2 hard-boiled eggs, halved
sea salt

TO SERVE
1 handful of Indonesian prawn crackers (*krupuk*)

1 Heat a frying pan over a medium-high heat, then add the peanuts and dry-roast until fragrant and starting to brown. Remove from the heat and roughly grind the peanuts in a food processor or blender – you want a fine powder with some chunky bits. Leave to one side.

2 Heat 1 tablespoon of the oil in a frying pan over a medium-high heat, then add the spice paste and cook, stirring occasionally, for 10–15 minutes until fragrant and the oil starts to rise to the surface. Add the lime juice, sugar, 250ml/9fl oz/1 cup water and season with salt. Tip in the ground peanuts and stir to combine. Bring to the boil, then remove from the heat and keep warm.

3 Meanwhile, heat the remaining 2 tablespoons of oil in a frying pan over a medium-high heat. Add the tofu pieces and shallow-fry for 3–4 minutes until golden brown all round. Remove the tofu with a slotted spoon and drain on paper towel. Leave to one side.

4 Bring a large saucepan of water to the boil, then tip in the green beans and cook for 3–4 minutes until tender but still crunchy. Remove from the water with kitchen tongs, refresh under running cold water and leave to one side. Bring the water back to the boil, add the bean sprouts and cook for about 20 seconds. Drain and leave to one side. Serve the tofu, green beans, bean sprouts, cucumber, carrot and eggs hot with Indonesian prawn crackers and the peanut sauce.

BRAISED PORK IN tomato sauce

Pork Afritada is a dish that was brought to the Philippines by the Spaniards. It is such a comfort food with a tomato base sauce, and one can quickly tell that it is a beautiful fusion dish that combines Asian ingredients (in this case, primarily, fish sauce) and the Western influence of using tomato as the base sauce.

SERVES 4
PREPARATION TIME 20 minutes
COOKING TIME 50 minutes to
  1 hour

3 plum tomatoes
2 tbsp sunflower oil
600g/1lb 5oz pork shoulder,
  excess fat removed and
  meat cut into chunky
  cubes
1 tbsp achiote seeds
2 garlic cloves, chopped
1 onion, chopped
1 red pepper, deseeded and
  cut into chunks
2 carrots, cut into chunks
4 floury potatoes, peeled
  and cut into quarters
1 tbsp tomato purée/paste
1 tbsp fish sauce
2 bay leaves
100g/3½oz frozen green
  peas
sea salt and freshly ground
  black pepper

TO SERVE
1 recipe quantity Boiled
  Long-Grain Rice (*see
  page 237*)

1 Score a cross on the base of each tomato, put them in a heatproof bowl and cover with boiling water. Leave to stand for a few seconds until the skin starts to curl. Drain and put in cold water, then peel off the skins, cut into quarters and set aside.

2 Heat 1 tablespoon of the oil in a big casserole pot over a medium-high heat, tip in half the pork and sear for 2 minutes, or until slightly brown. Remove the pork from the casserole using a slotted spoon and drain on paper towels. Repeat with the remaining pork, searing it in the oil left in the pot.

3 Discard the oil in the pot and add the remaining 1 tablespoon of sunflower oil in the same casserole pot over medium heat, then tip in the achiote seeds and stir until the oil turns red. Remove from the heat and leave to stand for about 1–2 minutes, or until the oil turns more red, then remove the seeds with a fine-mesh strainer spoon.

4 Make sure the pot is over a medium-high heat, then add the garlic, onion and red pepper and cook for about 2 minutes until softened. Add the pork, then stir and cook for 10–15 minutes, or until cooked through. Add in the carrots and potatoes, stir to combine, then add the tomato quarters, tomato purée, fish sauce and bay leaves and stir to mix well. Add 200ml/7fl oz/scant 1 cup of water, then bring to the boil for a few seconds and season with salt and black pepper.

5 Cover with the lid, reduce the heat and simmer for 25 minutes, stirring occasionally. Just 5 minutes before the cooking time ends, add the green peas and stir to combine. Remove the bay leaves; transfer to a serving bowl and serve with boiled rice.

CHICKEN BALL NOODLE SOUP

SERVES **4**
PREPARATION TIME **30 minutes**
COOKING TIME **30 minutes,**
    plus making the stock

500g/1lb 2oz skinless,
    boneless chicken breasts
1 tsp sea salt
1 tsp granulated sugar
4 tbsp cornflour/cornstarch
1 tsp ground white pepper
6 garlic cloves, peeled
1 onion, roughly chopped
2cm/¾in piece of fresh
    ginger, peeled and roughly
    chopped
1 tbsp sunflower oil
1 recipe quantity Chicken
    Stock (*see page 232*)
350g/12oz cooked rice
    vermicelli (*see page 238*)
2 spring onions/scallions,
    finely chopped
1 small handful of coriander/
    cilantro leaves, roughly
    chopped

TO SERVE
2 tbsp Fried Shallots (*see
    page 235*)
Sambal (*see page 236*)

Bakso is its native Indonesian name. This is a comfort food that always tops the list for any age group. You can use other meat, such as beef or pork, if you like – they taste just as nice.

1 Cut the chicken breasts into bite-size pieces, then transfer to a food processor. Blend to a paste and then transfer to a large bowl.

2 In a jug or small bowl, mix together the salt, sugar, cornflour and 3 tablespoons of cold water, then slowly stir into the chicken paste and mix until well combined. Season with the white pepper.

3 Using a teaspoon, scoop up some of the paste and shape it into a small ball of about 3cm/1¼in in diameter. It doesn't have to be perfectly round. Place the ball on a plate, then continue until all the paste has been used. You will get around 20–25 balls. Cover the chicken balls with cling film/plastic wrap and leave to one side.

4 Put the garlic, onion and ginger into a food processor (or use a pestle and mortar) and blend (or crush) together to a smooth paste. Heat a frying pan over a medium heat, add the oil and the paste and cook for about 5 minutes, or until fragrant. Remove from the heat.

5 Bring the chicken stock to the boil in a large saucepan. Stir in the cooked paste. Add the chicken balls, reduce the heat to low and simmer for about 5 minutes, or until they are cooked and float to the surface.

6 Meanwhile, divide the cooked rice vermicelli into deep soup bowls, then using a slotted spoon, remove the chicken balls from the stock and divide into the bowls of noodles. Sprinkle over the spring onions, coriander and fried shallots and drizzle over the shallot oil (see the recipe on page 235). Bring the chicken stock to a vigorous boil, then ladle it over the noodles. Serve immediately with the sambal on the side.

CITRUS-CURED TUNA & TOMATO SALAD

SERVES 4
PREPARATION TIME 20 minutes,
plus 25 minutes curing
time

500g/1lb 2oz skinless,
boneless tuna steaks
2 tbsp lime juice
2 tbsp lemon juice
2 tsp granulated sugar
1 garlic clove, grated
5mm/¼in piece of fresh
ginger, peeled and grated
1 green bird's eye chilli,
deseeded and finely diced
1 small red onion, finely
chopped
2 spring onions/scallions,
finely sliced
8 cherry tomatoes,
quartered
1 small handful of coriander/
cilantro leaves, roughly
chopped
sea salt and freshly ground
black pepper

Known as Kinilaw in the Philippines, this dish is similar to Ceviche and is usually served as a side dish. The combination of raw fish with all the other aromatic ingredients makes it a very refreshing starter, especially during the summer months. Vinegar is often used to partially cook the fish, but I have substituted it with lime and lemon juice, as I love the freshness they bring to the dish.

1 Place the tuna on a chopping/cutting board and cut against the grain into 5mm/¼in slices. Put in a bowl, season with salt and pepper and leave to one side.

2 Mix the lime juice, lemon juice, sugar and a pinch of salt in a small bowl until the sugar is dissolved. Stir in the garlic, ginger, chilli and onion, then pour the sauce over the tuna slices. Toss the tuna until well coated with the dressing, cover with cling film/plastic wrap and leave to marinate in the refrigerator for about 10 minutes.

3 Remove the tuna from the refrigerator and add the spring onions and cherry tomatoes to the bowl. Return to the refrigerator to marinate for a further 5 minutes, then remove and leave to stand at room temperature for 10 minutes before serving. Serve with the coriander sprinkled over.

BALINESE FISH SATAY

MAKES **16**
PREPARATION TIME **45 minutes**
COOKING TIME **about 45 minutes**

550g/1lb 4oz skinless, boneless white fish fillets, such as cod, haddock, snapper or whiting
1 recipe quantity Sate Lilit Ikan Spice Paste (*see page 229*)
20g/¾oz freshly grated coconut (*see page 240*) or desiccated/dried shredded coconut
1 tbsp clear honey
16 lemongrass stalks, outer leaves and stalk ends removed
sunflower oil for oiling
sea salt

TO SERVE
Sambal Matah (*see page 236*)

These satays are great served as party food. They offer something different from the usual beef or chicken satay and are delicious served with Sambal Matah, a Balinese sambal that is unique because the ingredients are sliced instead of ground to a paste.

1 Cut the fish fillets into bite-size pieces, then transfer to a food processor. Blend to a smooth paste and transfer to a bowl. Add the spice paste, coconut, honey and a pinch of salt to the bowl and mix until thoroughly combined.

2 Prepare a bowl of slightly salted water. Moisten one hand with the salted water to avoid the fish paste sticking, gather up the fish paste and shape into a ball. Pick up the ball, then slam it down into the bowl a few times until the mixture is glossy and the texture is smooth and springy. Remoisten your hand as necessary.

3 Place 2 heaped tablespoons of the mixture into the centre of a moistened palm. Use the back of the spoon to flatten the mixture into a 5cm/2in circle, then slightly close your hand and place the root end of a lemongrass stalk onto the mixture. Mould the paste around the lemongrass, covering only half the stick. Place the fish satay on a plate and repeat until all the ingredients are used. Brush the fish satay mixture with oil until coated all round.

4 Pour some oil into a ridged griddle pan or heavy-based frying pan over a medium-high heat, then use a paper towel to grease the pan evenly and soak up any excess oil. Griddle a batch of 5 or 6 satays for 7–10 minutes on each side until golden brown and cooked through. Transfer to a serving plate and keep warm. Oil the pan again, if required, and repeat until all the satays are cooked. Serve hot with the Sambal Matah.

SPICY tOFU

It couldn't be simpler to make this Indonesia-style street food. Originating from West Java, this snack, which is served with a pungent, sweet, sour and spicy sauce, is simply irresistible. For a true Javanese experience, you could replace the firm tofu with tofu puffs, which can be found in Asian supermarkets. They provide a crunchy layer and their spongy centre soaks up all the flavours.

SERVES **4**
PREPARATION TIME **20 minutes**
COOKING TIME **20 minutes**

200ml/7fl oz/scant 1 cup
  sunflower oil
350g/12oz firm tofu, cut
  into bite-size cubes
1 small cucumber, halved
  lengthways, deseeded and
  sliced into chunks

DRESSING
3 shallots, sliced
2 red bird's eye chillies,
  deseeded and chopped
2 green bird's eye chillies,
  deseeded and chopped
1 garlic clove, finely chopped
3 tbsp grated palm sugar or
  soft light brown sugar
2 tbsp lime juice or 1 recipe
  quantity Tamarind Water
  (*see page 242*)

1 To make the dressing, put the shallots, red and green chillies and garlic in a mortar or food processor and pound with a pestle or blend into a rough paste. Transfer to a bowl. In a separate bowl, mix together the sugar with 2 tablespoons hot water until dissolved. Stir in the lime juice and then the prepared chilli paste. Leave to one side.

2 Heat the oil in a deep, heavy-based saucepan or wok to 180°C/350°F or until a small piece of bread turns brown in 15 seconds. Gently slide the tofu into the oil and fry in batches for 10 minutes, or until lightly golden brown. Remove the tofu from the oil, using a slotted spoon, and drain on paper towels. Divide the tofu and cucumber onto four plates. Drizzle over the dressing and serve at room temperature.

Indonesian Sweet Pancakes

MAKES 5–6
PREPARATION TIME 20 minutes,
  plus 25–30 minutes
  resting time
COOKING TIME 45 minutes

75g/2½oz/scant ⅔ cup
  self-raising/self-rising flour
55g/2oz/scant ⅓ cup rice
  flour
1 tsp baking powder
½ tsp instant yeast powder
100g/3½oz/scant ½ cup
  caster/superfine sugar
1 egg
125ml/4fl oz/½ cup coconut
  milk

FILLING
75g/2½oz/½ cup raw cashew
  nuts
40g/1½oz butter or
  margarine, softened and
  cut into cubes, plus extra
  for greasing
55g/2oz/¼ cup granulated
  sugar
75g/2½oz/scant 1 cup
  desiccated/dried shredded
  coconut

Known as Martabak Manis, these pancakes can be eaten either savoury or sweet. This classic, sweet version uses coconut milk, which makes them both fragrant and light. For a less traditional version, they could be filled with chocolate chips, fruit or anything else you'd like.

1 Combine the self-raising flour, rice flour, baking powder, instant yeast powder and caster sugar in a mixing bowl. Crack in the egg and stir until combined. In a separate jug or bowl, mix together the coconut milk and 100ml/3½fl oz/⅓ cup + 2 tbsp water, then slowly pour into the dry ingredients and mix to a smooth batter. Leave at room temperature for 25–30 minutes.

2 Meanwhile, heat a frying pan over a medium-high heat, then add the cashew nuts and dry-roast until fragrant and starting to brown. Remove from the heat and roughly grind in a food processor or blender – you want a fine powder with some chunky bits.

3 Heat a 18cm/7in heavy-based frying pan over a medium heat and lightly grease with butter. Spoon a ladleful of the batter into the centre of the pan, then swirl the pan to cover the base with the batter. Cook the pancake for 3–4 minutes, or until little bubbles start to form on the surface.

4 Put a knob/pat of the butter on the pancake and sprinkle over 2 teaspoons of the granulated sugar, 1 tablespoon of the ground cashews and 1 tablespoon of the desiccated coconut. Use a spatula to check the pancake is golden brown underneath, then transfer to a plate and fold it in half. Leave to one side and keep warm while you make the remaining 4 or 5 pancakes. Serve hot.

Steamed Rice cakes

SERVES 12
PREPARATION TIME 20 minutes,
  plus 30 minutes resting
  time
COOKING TIME 15 minutes

300g/10½oz/generous
  1⅔ cups rice flour
150g/5½oz/scant 1¼ cups
  self-raising/self-rising flour
1 tbsp baking powder
1 tsp instant yeast powder
190g/6¾oz/heaped ¾ cup
  caster/superfine sugar
a pinch of sea salt
400ml/14fl oz/generous 1½
  cups coconut milk
1½ tsp green tea powder,
  for colouring
2 tbsp freshly grated
  coconut (*see page 240*) or
  desiccated/dried shredded
  coconut, to serve
grated palm sugar or soft
  light brown sugar, to serve
  (optional)

Steamed Rice Cakes, known as Puto, is a traditional
Filipino dessert. The most popular natural colouring for
these is extract of Pandan leaves, which is usually used for
its bright green colour and its sweet fragrance. However,
I've used green tea powder because it is much easier to
prepare. Usually eaten as an afternoon snack with a cup of
tea or coffee, they are also often served during breakfast.

1 Combine the rice flour, self-raising flour, baking powder, instant
  yeast powder, sugar and salt in a mixing bowl. Add the coconut milk
  and 3 tablespoons water and stir until the sugar is dissolved. Pour
  half of the mixture into a separate bowl, add the green tea powder
  and mix well. Leave both the green and white mixtures to stand at
  room temperature for 30 minutes.

2 Divide the white mixture into six individual muffin moulds or
  100ml/3½fl oz/generous ⅓ cup ramekins. Repeat with the green
  mixture to give a total of 12 rice cakes.

3 Arrange the moulds in a bamboo or electric steamer and steam for
  15 minutes, or until the cakes are nicely risen. Depending on the
  size of the steamer, you may need to cook the rice cakes in batches.
  Serve hot or cold with the coconut scattered over and a sprinkling
  of sugar, if you like.

MALAYSIA & SINGAPORE

Malaysian food is like an array of delicious foods that reflects the country's different ethnic backgrounds – Malay, Chinese, Indian, Nyonya, Eurasian and the indigenous people of Borneo. Beef Rendang (*see page 116*) is a truly delicious example of Malay cuisine, and the spicy, sweet, sour and salty tastes in Penang Assam Laksa (*see page 118*) show the natural fusion of Malay and Chinese ingredients and cooking techniques. The spice trade in the 15th century brought many different exotic spices to Malaysia, including cardamom, cinnamon, clove and star anise, and these are still popular spices to cook with and are all used to make Malaysian Chicken Red Curry (*see page 108*), for example.

Singapore was an important port for the spice trade during the British occupation, and this, along with the different ethnic groups, has also resulted in a rich and strong food culture. Along with the different spices, such as cinnamon, coriander, cumin, fennel and five-spice powder, other flavourings often used are chilli, ginger, garlic, shallots, soy sauce and shrimp paste, as seen in the mouth-watering Singaporean Chilli Crab (*see page 125*). Another dish that provides a delicious all-round example of the flavours and style of Singaporean food, and the strong influence of Chinese cuisine, is Pork & Mushroom Noodles (*see page 112*).

SERVES **4**
PREPARATION TIME **20 minutes,**
**plus 40 minutes marinating
and soaking time**
COOKING TIME **30–35 minutes**

700g/1lb 9oz chicken
    drumsticks or 500g/1lb 2oz
    skinless, boneless chicken
    thighs, cut into bite-size
    pieces
1 tbsp sesame oil
1 tbsp oyster sauce
2 tbsp light soy sauce
2 tbsp dark soy sauce
1 tbsp Shaoxing rice wine
1 tbsp clear honey
3cm/1¼in piece of fresh
    ginger, peeled and finely
    grated, pulp discarded,
    reserving the juice
350g/12oz/1¾ cups Long-
    Grain Rice, soaked and
    rested (*see page 237*)
2 tbsp sunflower oil
4 dried Chinese
    mushrooms, soaked,
    drained and sliced into
    thin strips (*see page 242*)
2 spring onions/scallions,
    finely sliced
2 red bird's eye chillies,
    finely sliced, to serve
    (optional)
freshly ground black pepper

CLAYPOT CHICKEN RICE

If you can, cook this dish the traditional way in a claypot. You will get to enjoy a particularly crunchy layer of rice, which will form at the base and is an important characteristic of the dish. The combination of fluffy and crunchy rice, chicken generously coated in a tasty sauce and the earthy flavour of Chinese mushrooms makes this a mouth-watering and satisfying dish.

1 If using chicken drumsticks, rinse the drumsticks under running cold water and pat dry with paper towels. Remove the skin and then, using a large chef's knife, cut each drumstick into 2 pieces through the bone. Put the drumstick pieces or thighs, if using, into a large bowl and add the sesame oil, oyster sauce, light and dark soy sauces, rice wine, honey and ginger juice and season with pepper. Toss until each piece of chicken is well coated with the marinade, then cover with cling film/plastic wrap and leave to marinate at room temperature for 30 minutes.

2 Put the rice in a claypot or deep, heavy-based saucepan. Place the pot over a high heat, pour in 455ml/16fl oz/scant 2 cups water and bring to the boil. Stir well, then reduce the heat to low, cover and simmer for 10 minutes.

3 Meanwhile, heat the sunflower oil in a frying pan over a medium-high heat. Add the mushrooms and stir-fry for 1 minute, then remove with a slotted spoon and leave to one side. Add the marinated chicken to the pan, reserving the marinade, and cook, stirring occasionally, for 10–12 minutes until almost cooked and browned. Leave to one side.

4 After the rice has simmered for 10 minutes and the liquid is almost absorbed, spread the chicken pieces and mushrooms on top of the rice. Cover and continue to cook over a very low heat for another 15 minutes, or until the chicken is cooked through. Add the reserved marinade and cook for 4–5 minutes, then add in the spring onions and cook for a further 1 minute. Serve immediately with the chilli slices sprinkled over, if you like.

HAINANESE CHICKEN RICE

SERVES 4–6
PREPARATION TIME 1 hr 15 mins
COOKING TIME 45 minutes

1 x 1.5kg/3lb 5oz whole
  chicken
1 tbsp sunflower oil
2cm/¾in piece of fresh
  ginger, peeled and finely
  chopped
1 garlic clove, finely chopped
2 shallots, thinly sliced
½ tsp sea salt
350g/12oz/1¾ cups Long-
  Grain Rice, soaked and
  rested (*see page 237*)
3 lemongrass stalks, outer
  leaves and stalk ends
  removed and crushed
1 spring onion/scallion, finely
  chopped, to serve
1 small cucumber, halved
  lengthways, deseeded and
  sliced, to serve

CHILLI DIPPING SAUCE
5 large red chillies, chopped
2 red bird's eye chillies,
  deseeded and chopped
3 garlic cloves, chopped
1cm/½in piece of fresh
  ginger, peeled and grated
1¼ tbsp granulated sugar
2 tbsp light soy sauce
½ tsp sea salt
2 tbsp lime juice

BASIL DIPPING SAUCE
55g/2oz Thai basil leaves
1 green bird's eye chilli,
  deseeded and roughly
  chopped
4 garlic cloves, roughly chopped
1 tsp sunflower oil
sea salt

1 To make the chilli dipping sauce, put the chillies, garlic and ginger into a food processor and blend to a smooth paste. Transfer to a small bowl, add the sugar and stir until dissolved. Stir in the soy sauce, salt and lime juice and leave to one side.

2 To make the basil dipping sauce, put the Thai basil leaves, chilli and garlic into a food processor and blend to a smooth paste. Transfer to a small bowl, add a pinch of salt and stir in the oil. Leave to one side.

3 Rinse the chicken thoroughly inside and out under running cold water and pat dry inside and out with paper towels.

4 Half fill a large, heavy-based saucepan with water and bring to the boil over a high heat. Add the chicken, breast-side down, and boil for about 20 seconds. Reduce the heat to low, cover and simmer for 15 minutes. Skim any scum or fat from the surface, turn over the chicken, cover again and continue to cook for 10–15 minutes until the chicken is cooked. When the tip of a sharp knife is inserted into the thickest part of the meat, the juices should run clear.

5 Remove the chicken from the stock and leave until it is cool enough to handle. Leave the chicken stock in the saucepan but turn off the heat. Using a pair of poultry scissors or a large sharp knife, cut the chicken into 12–18 pieces, as preferred.

6 Meanwhile, heat the oil in a saucepan over a medium-high heat. Add the ginger, garlic and shallots and cook, stirring occasionally, for 5–7 minutes until fragrant but not coloured. Add the salt and rice and stir-fry for 1–2 minutes. Pour in 455ml/16fl oz/scant 2 cups of the chicken stock and add the lemongrass. Bring to the boil, then stir with a wooden spoon to prevent the rice sticking to the base of the pan. Reduce the heat to low, cover and simmer gently for 20 minutes.

7 Remove the pan from the heat, leaving the lid tightly closed, and leave to steam for 10–15 minutes until cooked. Fluff the rice with a fork and discard the lemongrass. Meanwhile, bring the remaining chicken stock to the boil.

8 Divide the rice onto individual plates and top with the chicken pieces. Ladle the chicken stock into individual bowls and sprinkle over the spring onions. Serve with the cucumber, chilli dipping sauce, basil dipping sauce and the chicken stock on the side.

CHICKEN & PRAWN LAKSA

SERVES **4–6**
PREPARATION TIME **45 minutes**
COOKING TIME **1 hour
30 minutes, plus cooking
the noodles**

600g/1lb 5oz chicken
drumsticks, skin and excess
fat removed
500g/1lb 2oz raw, peeled
large king prawns/jumbo
shrimp, deveined (*see
page 241*)
2 tbsp sunflower oil
2 sprigs curry leaves
(optional)
1 recipe quantity Laksa Spice
Paste (*see page 228*)
500ml/17fl oz/2 cups
coconut milk
300g/10½oz cooked fresh
egg noodles or 250g/9oz
dried fine egg noodles (*see
page 238*)
200g/7oz cooked dried rice
vermicelli (*see page 238*)
100g/3½oz Chinese long
beans or green beans,
trimmed and cut into
5cm/2in lengths
200g/7oz/2 cups bean
sprouts
200g/7oz firm tofu, fried
2 hard-boiled eggs,
quartered
sea salt

TO SERVE
Chilli Paste (*see page 234
– optional*)

1 Pour 1.5 litres/52fl oz/6 cups water into a large, heavy-based
saucepan and bring to the boil over a medium-high heat. Add the
chicken drumsticks and boil for about 10 minutes, then reduce
the heat to low, cover and simmer for about 10 minutes. Skim
off any scum or fat from the surface and continue to simmer for
10–15 minutes until cooked. When the tip of a sharp knife is
inserted into the thickest part of the meat, the juices should run
clear. Remove the drumsticks, using a pair of tongs, and leave to
one side until cool enough to handle. Leave the chicken stock
simmering in the saucepan.

2 Cut the meat off the drumsticks, then shred or slice the meat.
Cover with cling film/plastic wrap and leave to one side. Return the
bones to the stock, reduce the heat to low and continue to simmer
for 30 minutes.

3 Meanwhile, transfer 300ml/10½fl oz/scant 1¼ cups of the chicken
stock into a separate saucepan and bring to the boil over a medium-
high heat. Add the prawns and cook until they turn pink and are
cooked through. Using a slotted spoon, remove the prawns from
the stock, drain on paper towel and leave to one side. Return the
prawn-flavoured stock to the main pan of simmering chicken stock.

4 Heat the oil in a frying pan over a medium-high heat. Add the curry
leaves, if using, and fry for 1–2 minutes until fragrant. Add the spice
paste and cook gently, stirring occasionally, for 10–15 minutes until
fragrant and the oil starts to rise to the surface. Remove the curry
leaves from the pan, then pour the paste into the stock. Add the
coconut milk to the stock and season with salt.

5 Divide the warm, cooked egg noodles and rice vermicelli into deep
soup bowls. Bring a saucepan of water to the boil and blanch the
Chinese long beans for about 2 minutes then, using a pair of tongs,
remove the beans and divide into the bowls of noodles. Return the
water to the boil and blanch the bean sprouts for about 20 seconds.
Drain and divide into the bowls with the noodles and beans.

6 Divide the shredded chicken, the prawns, fried tofu and hard-boiled
eggs into the bowls on top of the bean sprouts. Bring the stock to a
vigorous boil, then ladle into the bowls. Serve immediately with
chilli paste on the side, if you like.

MALAYSIAN CHICKEN RED CURRY

SERVES 4–6
PREPARATION TIME 45 minutes,
plus 2 hours 30 minutes
marinating and resting
time
COOKING TIME 2 hours
15 minutes

1kg/2lb 4oz chicken
drumsticks, skin and
excess fat removed
1 tbsp ground turmeric
500ml/17fl oz/2 cups
sunflower oil, for
deep-frying
2 red onions, sliced into rings
4 green cardamoms
2 star anise
2 cloves
6cm/2½in cinnamon stick
1 recipe quantity Ayam
Masak Merah Spice Paste
(*see page 226*)
4 tomatoes, skinned and
quartered (*see page 242*)
2 tbsp lime juice or 1 recipe
quantity Tamarind Water
(*see page 242*)
2 tbsp tomato purée/paste
3 tbsp tomato ketchup
1 tsp dark soy sauce
3 tbsp granulated sugar
sea salt

TO SERVE
1 recipe quantity Boiled
Long-Grain Rice (*see page
237 – optional*)

When I was learning to cook, my mum shared with me a tip that she said would ensure my aromatic curries will always be a success: *empat sekawan* or the 'four buddies' – star anise, green cardamom, clove and cinnamon. Used here with the spice paste, I guarantee you that this will be one of the most aromatic and delicious red curries you will ever eat.

1 Season the chicken drumsticks with salt and lightly coat with the turmeric. Cover with cling film/plastic wrap and leave to marinate in the refrigerator for about 2 hours.

2 Remove the chicken from the refrigerator and leave to stand at room temperature for about 30 minutes before deep-frying. Heat 455ml/16fl oz/scant 2 cups of the oil in a wok or deep, heavy-based saucepan to 180°C/350°F or until a small piece of bread turns brown in 15 seconds. Fry the chicken drumsticks in batches for about 15 minutes until they turn golden brown. Don't overcrowd the wok or pan, as this will lower the temperature of the oil. Remove the drumsticks from the oil with kitchen tongs and drain on paper towels or a wire cooling rack and leave to one side.

3 Heat the remaining oil in a saucepan over a medium heat. Add the onions, cardamoms, star anise, cloves and cinnamon stick and cook until the onion is soft and translucent. Add the spice paste and cook gently, stirring occasionally, for 10–15 minutes until fragrant and the oil starts to rise to the surface. Stir in the tomatoes and cook for about a further 5 minutes.

4 Add the lime juice and 100ml/3½fl oz/generous ⅓ cup water and bring to the boil. Reduce the heat to low and simmer for 15 minutes. Stir in the tomato purée, tomato ketchup, soy sauce and sugar and season with salt.

5 Add the fried chicken pieces to the pan and push around the pan with a wooden spoon until they are well coated with the sauce. Increase the heat to high and bring to the boil, then reduce the heat to medium-low, cover and cook, stirring occasionally, for 40 minutes, or until the chicken is cooked through and the sauce has thickened. Serve immediately with boiled rice, if you like.

NYONYA FRIED CHICKEN

SERVES 4–6
PREPARATION TIME **30 minutes,**
plus minimum 4 hours
30 minutes marinating
and resting time
COOKING TIME **20 minutes**

5 shallots, roughly chopped
1 tbsp ground coriander
1 tsp ground cumin
1 tsp ground turmeric
1 egg yolk
1 tbsp cornflour/cornstarch
2 tsp honey
1¼ tsp sea salt
2cm/¾in piece of fresh
ginger, peeled and finely
grated, pulp discarded,
reserving the juice
1kg/2lb 4oz chicken
drumsticks, excess fat
removed
500ml/17fl oz/2 cups
sunflower oil, for
deep-frying
freshly ground black pepper

DIPPING SAUCE
1 tbsp Worcestershire sauce
1 tbsp granulated sugar
1 tbsp light soy sauce
1 red bird's eye chilli,
deseeded and finely sliced
juice of 1 lime

TO SERVE
1 recipe quantity Boiled
Long-Grain Rice (*see page
237*)

This is a fantastic, easy-to-make Baba Nyonya-influenced dish. If you can, marinate the chicken overnight so you get to enjoy the full impact of flavours and especially tender chicken. The Worcestershire sauce used in the dipping sauce is an example of the colonial influences in Malaysian cuisine.

1 Put the shallots in a mortar and pestle or a food processor and blend to a smooth paste. Transfer to a large bowl and add the coriander, cumin, turmeric, egg yolk, cornflour, honey, sea salt and ginger juice and season with pepper. Stir to mix well. Tip in the chicken drumsticks and toss until each piece of chicken is well coated in the marinade. Cover with cling film/plastic wrap and leave to marinate in the refrigerator for at least 4 hours or, for an even better flavour, overnight.

2 Remove the chicken from the refrigerator and leave to stand at room temperature for about 30 minutes before deep-frying. Meanwhile, in a small bowl, mix together the dipping sauce ingredients and leave to one side.

3 Heat the oil in a deep, heavy-based saucepan to 180°C/350°F or until a small piece of bread turns brown in 15 seconds. Gently slide half the drumsticks into the oil and fry for 10 minutes, or until the meat is cooked through and the skin crispy. Remove the drumsticks with kitchen tongs and drain on paper towels or a wire cooking rack, keeping warm. Make sure the oil is still hot, then repeat with the remaining drumsticks. Alternatively, bake the drumsticks in a preheated oven, 200°C/400°F/Gas 6, for about 20 minutes until cooked through. Serve hot with boiled rice and the dipping sauce on the side.

PORK & MUSHROOM noodles

There are many ways of serving noodles, but the two most common are either in a soup or tossed in a sauce (with a soup served on the side). The latter is referred to as 'dry' noodles and Bak Chor Mee is a great example. This dish is of southern China origin, and is popular in Singapore. Over time it has evolved, and one of the changes is serving it with sambal – a chilli-based sauce.

SERVES 4
PREPARATION TIME 20 minutes, plus 25 minutes soaking time
COOKING TIME 15 minutes, plus cooking the noodles

1 tbsp sunflower oil
2 garlic cloves, finely chopped
30g/1oz dried mushrooms, such as shiitake, porcini or Chinese mushrooms, soaked, drained and roughly chopped, and liquid reserved (*see page 242*)
350g/12oz minced/ground pork
150g/5½oz/1¼ cups bean sprouts or mixed sprouts
300g/10½oz cooked dried egg noodles (*see page 238*)
freshly ground black pepper

SAUCE
3 tsp clear honey
5 tbsp light soy sauce
2 tbsp dark soy sauce
1 tbsp sesame oil
4½ tsp balsamic vinegar

TO SERVE
Sambal (*see page 236 – optional*)
2 spring onions/scallions, sliced into thin strips lengthways

1 To make the sauce, combine all the ingredients with 2 tablespoons warm water in a small bowl. Season with pepper and set aside.

2 Heat the sunflower oil in a frying pan over a medium-high heat. Add the garlic and stir-fry for 1–2 minutes, or until fragrant. Add the mushrooms and stir-fry for 1 minute. Tip in the pork and break up any lumps. Add 5 tablespoons of the mushroom liquid, season with pepper and cook, stirring occasionally, for 5–7 minutes until the pork is cooked through. Remove from the heat and keep warm.

3 Bring a saucepan of water to the boil and blanch the bean sprouts for about 20 seconds. Divide the warm, cooked noodles onto serving dishes, then top with the blanched bean sprouts. Spoon the sauce over the noodles and bean sprouts, then spoon over the pork and mushroom mixture. Sprinkle over the spring onions, add 1 heaped teaspoon of sambal to each bowl, if using, and serve immediately.

BRAISED PORK RIBS

SERVES **4**
PREPARATION TIME **15 minutes**
COOKING TIME **2 hours
15 minutes**

800g/1lb 12oz pork ribs, cut lengthways into 4cm/1½in pieces
1 tbsp sunflower oil
4 garlic cloves, finely chopped
2 red chillies, deseeded and sliced
1cm/½in piece of fresh ginger, peeled and finely chopped
3 tbsp Chinese fermented soybean paste
1 tbsp Shaoxing rice wine
1 tbsp dark soy sauce
1 tbsp lime juice or ½ recipe quantity Tamarind Water (*see page 242*)
1 tsp honey

TO SERVE
400g/14oz cooked rice noodles (*see page 238*)
1 spring onion/scallion, thinly sliced on the diagonal

This is a dish that I will always remember eating as a child. My mum still makes it often, and always with more chilli than is normal to give the sauce a bigger kick. Barbecuing is a popular way to cook spare ribs, but another way, which I think is much better and use here, is braising – slowly cooking the ribs in a broth until the meat is so tender it almost falls off the bones.

1 Bring a large saucepan of water to the boil, then carefully tip in the pork ribs and poach for 1–2 minutes until sealed. Drain the ribs into a colander, rinse the ribs under running cold water to stop the cooking process and leave to one side.

2 Heat the oil in a large saucepan over a medium-high heat. Add the garlic, chillies and ginger and stir-fry for 2–3 minutes until fragrant but not coloured. Add the pork ribs and push around the pan until well coated with the spices. Add the soybean paste, rice wine, soy sauce, lime juice and honey and stir thoroughly.

3 Add 250ml/9fl oz/1 cup water to the pan and bring to the boil. Reduce the heat to low and simmer, covered, for 2 hours until the meat is very tender and almost falls apart. Sprinkle with the spring onion and serve immediately.

BEEF RENDANG

Beef Rendang is one of those classic curries where the extra effort of making the spice paste from scratch is absolutely worthwhile. Although a Rendang can be made with lamb or chicken, the rich and thick sauce goes especially well with beef.

SERVES 4–6
PREPARATION TIME 30 minutes
COOKING TIME about 2 hours 45 minutes

55g/2oz freshly grated coconut (*see page 240*) or 40g/1½oz/scant ½ cup desiccated/dried shredded coconut
3 tbsp sunflower oil
1 recipe quantity Rendang Spice Paste (*see page 230*)
1kg/2lb 4oz casserole steak, trimmed of fat and cut into bite-size pieces
2 tbsp lime juice or 1 recipe quantity Tamarind Water (*see page 242*)
2 lemongrass stalks, outer leaves and stalk ends removed and crushed
5 kaffir lime leaves, bruised
2 tbsp grated palm sugar or soft light brown sugar
400ml/14fl oz/generous 1½ cups coconut milk
sea salt

TO SERVE
1 recipe quantity Boiled Long-Grain Rice (*see page 237*)

1 Heat a frying pan over a medium heat and dry-fry the coconut for 3–5 minutes until light golden brown, stirring occasionally. Leave to one side.

2 Heat the oil in a large casserole pot or a wok over a medium-high heat. Add the spice paste and cook gently, stirring occasionally, for 10–15 minutes until fragrant and the oil starts to rise to the surface. Tip the beef into the pan, stir until well coated, then cook for 5–10 minutes until sealed and beginning to brown.

3 Add the lime juice, lemongrass, kaffir lime leaves, sugar and coconut milk and season with salt. Bring to the boil, then reduce the heat to low and simmer, uncovered, for 2–2½ hours until tender and the meat is falling apart. During the last 45 minutes of cooking stir more frequently. When the liquid starts to thicken, add in the toasted coconut and mix well. Serve immediately with boiled rice.

PENANG ASSAM LAKSA

SERVES 4–6
PREPARATION TIME 1 hour
COOKING TIME 45 minutes,
plus cooking the noodles

700g/1lb 9oz whole
  mackerels or herrings,
  gutted, scaled and trimmed
  by your fishmonger
2 stalks Vietnamese
  coriander/cilantro
4–5 strips lime zest or
  tamarind peel
1 recipe quantity Assam
  Laksa Spice Paste (*see page 228*)
1 tbsp granulated sugar
4 tbsp lime juice or 2 tbsp
  lime juice and 1 recipe
  quantity Tamarind Water
  (*see page 242*)
500g/1lb 2oz cooked thick
  rice noodles, such as Lai
  Fun (*see page 238*)
sea salt

TOPPINGS
1 small cucumber, halved
  lengthways, deseeded and
  cut into matchsticks
2 wedges fresh pineapple,
  peeled and cut into strips
½ red onion, thinly sliced
1 handful of mint leaves
2–3 green bird's eye chillies,
  deseeded and finely sliced

TO SERVE
1 lime, cut into wedges

Assam Laksa is just one of the many variations of Laksa. You can use lime zest or tamarind peel – *asam gelugor* or *asam keping* – to add an extra level of sourness to the broth. The combination of flavours – saltiness, sourness and spiciness is a bold feature and makes Assam Laksa stand out from other variations.

1 Rinse the mackerels or herrings inside and out under running cold water and pat dry with paper towels. Pour 2 litres/70fl oz/8 cups water into a large saucepan over a high heat and bring to the boil. Add the fish and boil for a few seconds, then reduce the heat to low and cook for about 10 minutes. Remove the herrings from the simmering stock and leave to one side to cool.

2 Put the Vietnamese coriander and lime zest in a spice bag or secure in a piece of muslin/cheesecloth and add to the fish stock along with the spice paste, sugar and lime juice. Season with salt and simmer for about 25 minutes.

3 Meanwhile, using a fork, flake the fish, removing the bones and skin. Ten minutes before the end of making the stock, add the fish.

4 When ready to serve, drain the warm, cooked rice noodles and divide into deep soup bowls. Remove the spice bag from the stock and ladle the stock and fish over the noodles. Sprinkle over the topping ingredients and serve warm with lime wedges on the side.

SINGAPOREAN FISH BALL NOODLE SOUP

SERVES **4–6**
PREPARATION TIME **50 minutes,
   plus making the stock**
COOKING TIME **15 minutes**

800g/1lb 12oz boneless,
   skinless white fish fillets,
   such as pollock or cod
¼ tsp sea salt
4½ tsp cornflour/cornstarch
4 tbsp sunflower oil
6 garlic cloves, finely
   chopped
150g/5½oz/1¼ cups bean
   sprouts
350g/12oz cooked 3mm/⅛in
   or 5mm/¼in rice sticks
   (*see page 238*)
1 recipe quantity Chicken
   Stock (*see page 232*)
2 spring onions/scallions,
   finely chopped
freshly ground black pepper

DIPPING SAUCE
1 red chilli, deseeded
   and sliced
1 tsp lime juice
2 tbsp light soy sauce

1 Cut the fish fillets into bite-size pieces, then transfer to a food processor. Blend to a paste and then transfer to a large bowl. In a separate jug or bowl, mix together the salt, cornflour and 45ml/1½fl oz/3 tablespoons cold water, then slowly stir into the fish paste and mix until well combined. Season with pepper.

2 Prepare a small bowl of water and add a pinch of salt. Moisten one hand in the salted water to avoid the fish paste sticking, gather up the fish paste and shape into a ball. Pick up the ball, then slam it down into the bowl a few times until the mixture is glossy and the texture is smooth and springy. Remoisten your hand as necessary.

3 Use a teaspoon or melon baller to scoop up the fish paste and shape into a ball. It doesn't have to be perfectly round. Place the ball on a plate and continue until all the fish paste has been used. Cover the fish balls with cling film/plastic wrap and leave to one side. Meanwhile, to make the dipping sauce, mix together all the ingredients in a small bowl.

4 Heat the oil in a frying pan over a medium heat. Add the garlic and stir-fry for 1–2 minutes until fragrant and starting to brown. Remove the pan from the heat and leave to one side.

5 Bring a saucepan of water to the boil and blanch the bean sprouts for about 20 seconds. Divide the warm, cooked rice sticks into deep soup bowls, then top with the blanched bean sprouts.

6 Pour the chicken stock into a saucepan over a medium-high heat and bring to the boil. Add the fish balls, reduce the heat to low and cook in the simmering stock for 3–4 minutes until they float to the surface. Using a slotted spoon, remove the fish balls from the stock and divide into the bowls of noodles and bean sprouts. Sprinkle over the spring onions and fried garlic, and drizzle over the garlic oil. Bring the chicken stock to a vigorous boil, then ladle it over the noodles. Serve immediately with the dipping sauce on the side.

SERVES **4**
PREPARATION TIME **20 minutes,**
plus 1 hour 10 minutes
marinating and resting
time
COOKING TIME **10–15 minutes**

500g/1lb 2oz raw, unpeeled
large king prawns/jumbo
shrimp
3 tbsp Shaoxing rice wine
2 tbsp light soy sauce
2 spring onions/scallions, cut
into 5cm/2in pieces and
thinly sliced lengthways
2.5cm/1in piece of fresh
ginger, peeled and thinly
sliced
1 egg, beaten
freshly ground black pepper

TO SERVE
1 recipe quantity Boiled
Long-Grain Rice (*see page
237*)

DRUNKEN PRAWNS

The name itself gives a not-so-subtle hint that the prawns are cooked in a generous amount of alcohol. Chinese rice wine, Shaoxing, is widely used in Chinese cooking, as it enhances flavour and also imparts a very light, earthy fragrance.

1 Using a pair of kitchen scissors, trim from each prawn the feelers, rostrum, legs and the sharp end of the tail. Make a slit along the back of the prawn with a sharp knife and pull out the black vein with the tip of the knife or your fingers. Rinse the prawns under running cold water and pat dry with paper towels.

2 Arrange the prawns on a heatproof dish that will fit inside a wok or an electric steamer, if using. Pour over the rice wine and soy sauce and season with pepper. Cover with cling film/plastic wrap and leave to marinate in the refrigerator for 1 hour. Remove from the refrigerator and leave to stand at room temperature for about 10 minutes before cooking.

3 Place a round steamer rack with legs at least 2.5cm/1in tall inside a wok. Leaving a minimum gap of 1cm/½in below the steamer, add water to the wok and bring to the boil over a medium-high heat. Sprinkle the spring onions and ginger over the prawns, then set the dish on the rack and cover the wok. Steam for 10–15 minutes until the prawns turn pink and are cooked through. Keep an eye on the level of the water, adding more boiling water if necessary.

4 Two minutes before the end of cooking, pour over the beaten egg. Serve warm with boiled rice.

MALAYSIAN PRAWN FRITTERS & TOFU WITH BUTTERNUT SQUASH SAUCE

SERVES 4–6
PREPARATION TIME 45 minutes
to 1 hour
COOKING TIME 1 hour
30 minutes

150g/5½oz firm tofu, cut
into bite-size cubes
200g/7oz/2 cups mixed
sprouts or bean sprouts
1 small cucumber, quartered
lengthways, deseeded and
cut into matchsticks
200g/7oz Jerusalem
artichokes, water chestnuts
or jicama, peeled and cut
into matchsticks
3 hard-boiled eggs, halved

BUTTERNUT SQUASH SAUCE
200g/7oz butternut squash,
deseeded, peeled and cut
into bite-size pieces
100g/3½oz/scant ⅔ cup
unsalted macadamia nuts
4 shallots, roughly chopped
2 red chillies, deseeded and
roughly chopped
2 tbsp sunflower oil
3 tbsp grated palm sugar or
soft light brown sugar
1½ tsp sea salt
1 tbsp lime juice or ½ recipe
quantity Tamarind Water
(*see page 242*)

This Malaysian-style salad is an interesting collaboration of ingredients from different ethnic backgrounds: prawn fritters, known as Cucur Udang in Malay, are a truly authentic Malaysian food; the spices used are typical of those used in Indian cuisine; and the tofu comes from Chinese cuisine. Together, the different flavours and textures combine to make a wonderfully tasty fusion dish.

1 To make the butternut squash sauce, put the butternut squash in a saucepan of boiling water and cook for 10 minutes, or until tender. Drain, mash until very smooth and leave to one side.

2 Meanwhile, heat a frying pan over a medium-high heat, then add the macadamia nuts and dry-roast until fragrant and starting to brown. Remove from the heat and roughly grind in a food processor or blender – you want a fine powder with some chunky bits.

3 Put the shallots and chillies in a food processor or blender and blend to a smooth paste. Heat the oil in a saucepan over a medium-high heat. Add the chilli paste and cook for 10 minutes, or until fragrant, stirring occasionally.

4 Stir the mashed butternut squash, sugar and salt into the paste, then add the lime juice and 210ml/7½fl oz/generous ¾ cup water. Bring to the boil, then reduce the heat to low and simmer for 5–10 minutes until the sauce starts to thicken, stirring occasionally. Add the ground macadamia nuts and cook for a further 2–3 minutes. Leave to one side and keep warm.

5 To make the batter for the prawn fritters, mix together the flour, turmeric and chilli powder in a large mixing bowl. Season with salt and pepper, then gradually stir in 100ml/3½fl oz/generous ⅓ cup water to form a smooth, thick batter. Add the egg, prawns, spring onions and shallots and leave to one side.

6 Heat the oil in a deep, heavy-based saucepan to 180°C/350°F or until a small piece of bread turns brown in 15 seconds. Gently drop 2 heaped tablespoons of the batter into the oil and fry for

PRAWN FRITTERS

80g/2¾oz/scant ⅔ cup
  self-raising/self-rising flour
½ tsp ground turmeric
¼ tsp chilli powder
1 egg, beaten
250g/9oz raw, peeled large
  king prawns/jumbo shrimp,
  deveined (*see page 241*)
2 spring onions/scallions,
  finely chopped
3 shallots, thinly sliced
500ml/17fl oz/2 cups
  sunflower oil, for d
  eep-frying
sea salt and freshly ground
  black pepper

3–4 minutes until golden brown. You can fry several fritters at a time, as long as they are well spaced. Using a slotted spoon, remove the fritters from the oil and drain on paper towels. Repeat until all the batter is used, then slice the fritters into chunks and keep warm.

7 Bring the oil back to a temperature of 180°C/350°F. Deep-fry the tofu in batches for 3–4 minutes until the tofu is golden brown and crispy. Using a slotted spoon, remove the tofu from the oil and drain on paper towels, keeping warm until all the tofu is used.

8 Meanwhile, bring a small saucepan of water to the boil and blanch the mixed sprouts for about 20 seconds, then drain.

9 Divide the cucumber, Jerusalem artichokes, mixed sprouts, hard-boiled eggs, tofu and prawn fritters between plates. Ladle over the warm butternut squash sauce and serve immediately.

SINGAPOREAN CHILLI CRAB

SERVES 4
PREPARATION TIME 45 minutes
COOKING TIME 20–25 minutes

1.5kg/3lb 5oz uncooked
  brown or blue swimmer
  crabs, or crab claws,
  scrubbed
3 tbsp sunflower oil
1 recipe quantity Chilli Crab
  Spice Paste (see page 226)
2 tbsp tomato ketchup
2 tbsp chilli sauce
2 tbsp clear honey
3 tbsp light soy sauce

TO SERVE
1 recipe quantity Boiled
  Long-Grain Rice (see
  page 237)

This slightly sweet, hot and spicy dish is undoubtedly one of the most popular ways to prepare crabs in Singapore. Fresh, meaty crabs are essential. When choosing a crab, gently press on the underbelly – if it is firm, then it will be more meaty. If using crab claws and not whole crabs, make sure that you crack the shell slightly before cooking, so that the flesh soaks up all the sauce. The shells will also peel away more easily.

1 To prepare each crab, pull off the triangular bony tail flap and discard. Press your thumb under the rear end of the crab and lift the body away from the back shell. Discard the shell and remove and discard the stomach bag and the gills at the sides of the body. Rinse the crab flesh and claws under running cold water and pat dry with paper towel. Pull the 2 front claws from the bodies and then, using the back of a knife or a mallet, slightly crack the shell of each claw. Cut the crabs into quarters with a large-bladed knife. If using crab claws only, rinse under running cold water and crack the claws slightly using a large-bladed knife.

2 Heat the oil in a wok or large frying pan over a high heat. Add the spice paste and cook gently, stirring occasionally, for 10–15 minutes until fragrant and the oil starts to rise to the surface.

3 Meanwhile, combine the tomato ketchup, chilli sauce, honey and soy sauce in a small bowl. Add the sauce mixture to the wok or pan, then pour in 90ml/3fl oz/generous ⅓ cup water and bring to the boil.

4 Tip in the crab pieces and push around the wok or pan until well coated with the sauce. Cover, reduce the heat to low and simmer for 8–10 minutes until the crab pieces turn bright orange and are cooked through. Serve immediately with boiled rice.

MALAYSIAN COCONUT & LEMONGRASS-SCENTED RICE WITH SQUID SAMBAL

SERVES 4–6
PREPARATION TIME 1 hour, plus soaking and resting time
COOKING TIME 1 hour 15 mins

350g/12oz/1¼ cups long-grain rice, washed and rested
1 star anise
2 lemongrass stalks, outer leaves and stalk ends removed and crushed
3 pandan leaves, tied into a knot (optional)
2cm/¾in piece of fresh ginger, peeled and finely chopped
100ml/3½fl oz/generous ⅓ cup coconut milk
½ tsp sea salt
100g/3½oz/scant ⅔ cup raw, skinless peanuts
1 tsp granulated sugar
4–6 banana leaves (optional)
2 hard-boiled eggs, quartered
1 small cucumber, halved, deseeded and cut into chunks
80g/2¾oz Toasted Dried Anchovies (*see page 242*)

SQUID SAMBAL
4 tbsp sunflower oil
2 red onions, sliced into rings
1 recipe quantity Squid Spice Paste (*see page 230*)
800g/1lb 12oz squid, cut into rings (*see page 241*)
1 tbsp granulated sugar
2 tbsp lime juice or 1 recipe quantity Tamarind Water (*see page 242*)
sea salt

1 To make the Squid Sambal, heat the oil in a frying pan over a medium-high heat, then add the onions and cook until soft and translucent. Add the spice paste and cook gently, stirring occasionally, for 10–15 minutes until fragrant and the oil starts to rise to the surface. Tip in the squid, stir until well coated and cook for about 5 minutes. Add the sugar and season with salt, then add the lime juice and stir to combine. Bring to the boil, then reduce the heat to low and simmer, covered, for 45 minutes, or until the sauce thickens and turns a dark reddish brown. Leave to one side and keep warm.

2 Meanwhile, put the rice, star anise, lemongrass, pandan leaves, if using, ginger, coconut milk and salt in a large saucepan and pour in 300ml/10½fl oz/scant 1¼ cups water. Put the pan over a high heat and bring to the boil for about 20 seconds. Stir with a wooden spoon to prevent the rice sticking to the base of the pan, reduce the heat to low, cover, and simmer gently for 20 minutes.

3 Remove the pan from the heat, leaving the lid tightly closed, and leave to one side to steam for 10–15 minutes until cooked. Fluff the rice with a fork and discard the star anise, lemongrass and pandan leaves, if using. Leave to one side and keep warm.

4 While the sambal and rice are cooking, heat a frying pan over a medium-high heat, then add the peanuts and dry-roast until fragrant and starting to brown. Tip the peanuts onto a plate, sprinkle over the sugar and leave to cool.

5 Serve the rice on plates or banana leaves. Ladle the Squid Sambal over the rice and top with the eggs. To the side, heap the cucumber, toasted anchovies and sugared peanuts. Serve hot.

ROtI CANAI WItH DHAL CURRY

Roti Canai, also known as Roti Prata, is served at *mamak* stalls – the al fresco hawker places you find almost everywhere in Kuala Lumpur. They are normally made by flipping the dough in the air and flapping it on the work surface until it is very thin – a fantastic sight. While you might like to try this technique at home, here I suggest you rest the dough on the work surface and stretch it out as thinly as you can without it tearing.

SERVES 4–6
PREPARATION TIME **1 hour, plus minimum 7 hours resting time**
COOKING TIME **1 hour 40 minutes–2 hours**

1 tsp sea salt
1 egg
4½ tsp condensed milk
1 tbsp butter, melted
500g/1lb 2oz/4 cups plain/all-purpose flour, plus extra for dusting
55ml/1¾fl oz/scant ¼ cup sunflower oil, plus extra for brushing and kneading

DHAL CURRY
1 tbsp sunflower oil
3 sprigs of curry leaves, rinsed
2 dried chillies, rinsed
1 onion, roughly chopped
2 carrots, diced
1 tbsp garam masala
½ tsp ground ginger
1 tsp ground turmeric
1 tbsp tomato purée/paste
3 tomatoes, skinned and roughly chopped (*see page 242*)
250g/9oz drained, canned lentils or 120g/4¼oz/scant ⅔ cup green lentils, soaked overnight
sea salt and freshly ground black pepper

1 Mix the salt together with 190ml/6½fl oz/generous ¾ cup water in a small bowl and set aside. In a separate bowl, mix together the egg, condensed milk and melted butter until well combined. Put the flour into a large mixing bowl and make a well in the centre. Pour in the egg mixture. Then, gradually pour in the salted water and combine with the flour to form a soft dough. Cover with cling film/plastic wrap and leave at room temperature for about 30 minutes.

2 Turn the dough out onto a lightly floured surface and knead for 5 minutes until it is smooth and elastic. Flatten the dough and split in half. Divide each half into 4–5 equal portions and roll each piece into a ball. Brush the dough balls generously with oil, then place side by side on a well-oiled dish. Sprinkle over more oil, about 55ml/1¾fl oz/scant ¼ cup, and cover with cling film/plastic wrap. Leave to rest at room temperature for at least 6 hours, or for the best result, overnight.

3 Oil a clean working surface and generously oil your palms. Take a dough ball and flatten, then slowly work the dough outwards from around the edge to expand it. Use your fingers to slowly pull around the edge of the dough to stretch it out. Do this carefully so as not to tear the pastry. Continue until the dough is very thin and almost translucent. Sprinkle some oil over the pastry and fold the edges into the centre to form a square. Air will be trapped as you fold, which will help make the roti crispy and fluffy once cooked. Set aside on an oiled dish and continue until all the dough balls are used. Leave to rest for 20 minutes.

4 Heat a ridged griddle pan over a high heat. When hot, add a roti and cook for 5–6 minutes on each side until blisters and brown spots form. Remove from the pan to a clean surface and, using your hands, gently whack it a few times moving in a circle around the roti to fluff it up. Keep warm and repeat until all the dough balls are used. Meanwhile cook the dhal.

5 To make the dhal, heat the oil in a frying pan over a medium-high heat, then add the curry leaves and dried chillies and stir-fry until fragrant. Add the onion and stir-fry for 1–2 minutes until softened, then add the carrots and cook for 4–5 minutes until the carrots are tender, stirring occasionally. Add the garam masala, ginger, turmeric and tomato purée and stir to combine.

6 Tip in the tomatoes and lentils, then pour in 350ml/12fl oz/scant 1½ cups water. Bring to the boil for about 20 seconds, season with salt and pepper and then reduce the heat to low and cover. If using canned lentils simmer for 10–15 minutes and if using soaked lentils simmer for 30–45 minutes, or until the dhal is very soft, stirring occasionally. Serve the roti warm with the hot dhal curry.

NYONYA PINEAPPLE CURRY

SERVES **4**
PREPARATION TIME **30 minutes**
COOKING TIME **40 minutes**

1 ripe pineapple
1 tbsp sea salt
3 tbsp sunflower oil
2 star anise
6cm/2½in cinnamon stick
4 cloves
3 green cardamom pods
1 recipe quantity Pajeri
   Nanas Spice Paste (*see
   page 228*)
1–2 tbsp grated palm sugar
   or soft light brown sugar
30g/1oz/¼ cup dried
   cranberries, dried sour
   cherries, sultanas or raisins
sea salt

TO SERVE
1 recipe quantity Boiled
   Long-Grain Rice (*see page
   237*)

Pajeri Nanas, cooked the Nyonya way, simmers in a bright red, chilli-based sauce. An alternative way to make this dish is to use curry powder, but you miss out on the pureness of the fresh spices against the natural sweetness of the pineapple. Eaten with fluffy white rice, this aromatic dish with its slight hint of spiciness and natural sweetness of the pineapple seems like pure indulgence.

1 Cut the crown, about 2cm/¾in from the end, and the base off the pineapple, then, with the pineapple upright, carefully slice off the skin. Don't slice too deeply to remove the 'eyes', as good, edible flesh will be wasted. The 'eyes' on the pineapple run neatly in a spiral around the pineapple. To cut these out, place the pineapple horizontally and position a knife at an angle alongside 3 or 4 eyes. Cut a V-shape around the eyes, remove them and discard. Repeat, following the spiral, until all eyes are removed.

2 Rub the salt into the pineapple all round, then rinse under running cold water and pat dry with paper towel. This is to take away the acidity of the pineapple. Place the pineapple horizontally on a chopping/cutting board and cut it into 1cm/½in slices, then use a small ring cutter to remove the core from each piece. Leave the rings to one side and discard the cores.

3 Heat the oil in a large saucepan over a medium heat. Add the star anise, cinnamon stick, cloves and cardamom pods and cook for 3–4 minutes until fragrant, stirring occasionally. Add the spice paste and cook gently, stirring occasionally, for 10–15 minutes until fragrant and the oil starts to rise to the surface.

4 Add the pineapple slices and push around the pan with a wooden spoon until the pineapple is well coated with the paste. Pour in 170ml/5½fl oz/⅔ cup water and bring to the boil for about 20 seconds, then add the sugar and season with salt. Reduce the heat to low and simmer, covered, for 15 minutes until the pineapple is soft and the liquid starts to thicken.

5 Sprinkle the dried cranberries into the pan, cover and simmer for a further 2–3 minutes. Adjust the sweetness or sourness by adding a touch of salt and/or sugar, as required. Serve warm with boiled rice.

CRISPY PORK ROLLS

MAKES **12 rolls**
PREPARATION TIME **1 hour, plus 1
hour 20 minutes
marinating, resting and
cooling time**
COOKING TIME **25 minutes**

1 x 500g/1lb 2oz pork
  tenderloin
2 tbsp sesame oil
1 tsp five-spice powder
2 tsp clear honey
1 tbsp light soy sauce
¼ tsp ground white pepper
1 tbsp sesame seeds
2 tbsp cornflour/cornstarch
8 shallots, finely sliced
1 bean curd skin, wiped with
  a damp dish towel or 12
  Chinese spring roll
  wrappers, about 16 x
  18cm/6¼ x 7in in size
500ml/17fl oz/2 cups
  sunflower oil, for
  deep-frying

TO SERVE
mint, Thai basil and
  coriander/cilantro leaf salad
  (optional)

The ingredient that makes these rolls something really special is bean curd skin. There are two types available – one is opaque and a medium-yellow colour and the other is translucent and slightly oiled. It's best to use the translucent and slightly oiled one. If you cannot get bean curd skin, they are also delicious when made with Chinese spring roll wrappers, which are also known as egg roll wrappers.

1 Place the pork horizontally on a chopping/cutting board, then use a paring knife or a flexible, fine-bladed knife to trim off any fat and silver skin. To trim off the silver skin, slip the knife between the meat and the skin and slide the knife along the length of the tenderloin. Slice the pork into 5–10mm/¼–½in strips and put into a bowl.

2 Put the sesame oil, five-spice powder, honey, soy sauce, ground pepper, sesame seeds, cornflour and shallots in with the pork, then toss until the pieces of pork are well coated. Cover with cling film/plastic wrap and leave to marinate in the refrigerator for 1 hour.

3 Remove the pork from the refrigerator and leave to stand at room temperature for about 10 minutes before making the rolls. Meanwhile, lay the bean curd skin, if using, on a chopping/cutting board and cut into twelve 16 x 18cm/6¼ x 7in sheets.

4 Place 4 or 5 strips of the marinated pork horizontally along the centre of a bean curd sheet or spring roll wrapper, leaving a gap of about 1cm/½in around the edges. Fold the bottom edge over the filling, then fold in the two sides and roll up tightly. Lightly moisten the upper edge to seal, then place on a plate, cover with a damp dish towel and repeat until all the ingredients are used.

5 Place the pork rolls on a plate, then place in a bamboo or electric steamer and steam for 8–10 minutes until firm to the touch. Remove from the steamer and leave for about 10 minutes to cool slightly.

6 Heat the oil in a deep, heavy-based saucepan to 180°C/350°F or until a small piece of bread turns brown in 15 seconds. Gently slide 4 or 5 pork rolls into the oil and fry for 5 minutes, or until the pork rolls are golden brown. Drain the rolls on paper towels and keep warm while you fry the remaining pork rolls.

ADZUKI BEAN & BLACK GLUTINOUS RICE WITH COCONUT MILK

SERVES **4**
PREPARATION TIME **15 minutes,**
   plus soaking time and
   cooling
COOKING TIME **1½ hours**

200g/7oz dried adzuki
   beans, soaked overnight
150g/5½oz black glutinous
   rice, soaked overnight
2 pandan leaves, tied into
   a knot
150g/5½oz/generous ¾ cup
   caster/granulated sugar
350ml/12fl oz/scant 1½ cups
   coconut milk
2 tbsp granulated sugar
¼ tsp fine sea salt

When I crave for my childhood desserts, this has to be one of them. I remember growing up not being a big fan of black glutinous rice. Over time, I learned to love this grain, which is slightly chewy and crunchy at the same time, thus pairing perfectly with the soft cooked adzuki beans.

1 Pour 2 litres/70fl oz/8½ cups of water into a large pot or saucepan set over a medium-high heat, add the drained adzuki beans and black glutinous rice and the pandan leaves, then bring to the boil. Give it a quick stir, reduce the heat to low, cover with the lid and let it simmer for about 1 hour, or until the adzuki beans and black glutinous rice are soft and start to break up.

2 Stir in the caster/granulated sugar and simmer for a further 15–20 minutes, or until the liquid starts to thicken, then remove from the heat and leave it to cool. Once cool, discard the pandan leaves.

3 Meanwhile, pour the coconut milk into a separate saucepan, place over a medium heat and slowly bring to the boil. Remove from the heat, add the granulated sugar and salt and stir until the sugar is dissolved. Leave to one side to cool.

4 Divide the adzuki bean and black glutinous rice mixture into individual dessert glasses, filling each slightly more than half-full. Top up the glasses with the sugared coconut milk. Serve chilled or at room temperature.

MALAY-STYLE MADELEINES WITH COCONUT, LIME & CHOCOLATE

SERVES **4**
PREPARATION TIME **10 minutes**
COOKING TIME **30 minutes**

melted butter, for greasing
4 eggs
90g/3¼oz/heaped ⅓ cup
   caster/superfine sugar
¼ tsp baking powder
100g/3½oz/ heaped ¾ cup
   plain/all-purpose flour
1 tbsp lime juice
zest of 1 lime
3 tbsp desiccated/dried
   shredded coconut
2 tbsp chocolate sprinkles

Whenever the festive season is around the corner, whether it's Chinese New Year or Eid Mubarak, these little cakes are baked in most households. The texture is light and fluffy and they resemble French Madeleines. These are traditionally made using specific moulds of many different and beautiful shapes, such as flowers, fish and sea shells, but a mini muffin mould or Madeleine mould can also be used. I have given a little bit of a modern twist by adding desiccated coconut, a touch of lime and some chocolate sprinkles.

1 Preheat the oven to 200°C/400°F/Gas 6 and lightly grease a Madeleine or mini muffin mould with melted butter.

2 Using an electric mixer, beat the eggs and sugar together in a large mixing bowl and beat until thick and creamy. Add the baking powder and gradually fold in the flour using a spatula.

3 Add the lime juice, lime zest, desiccated coconut and chocolate sprinkles and gently fold through using a spatula.

4 Spoon the mixture into the prepared mould until each cup is three-quarters full. Put in the preheated oven and bake for about 7–8 minutes, or until golden brown. Remove from the oven and turn the madeleines out of the pan onto a wire cooling rack. Grease the mould again and repeat with the remaining batter and leave to cool completely.

SAGO PEARLS WITH COCONUT & CHOCOLATE SYRUP

SERVES 4–6
PREPARATION TIME **20 minutes**,
    plus 1 hour chilling
COOKING TIME **55 minutes**

300g/10½oz/scant 1⅓ cups
    small sago pearls
1 vanilla pod/bean
200ml/7fl oz/scant ¾ cup
    + 2 tbsp coconut milk
200g/7oz/heaped 1 cup palm
    sugar, grated, or soft light
    brown sugar
1 tsp unsweetened
    cocoa powder
sea salt

I love coconut milk with an added hint of saltiness, and this Malay dessert is a fantastic example of how well the sweet and salty combination works. Here you also have the combination of palm sugar and coconut milk, which provide big flavours in a very simple way.

1 Bring a large saucepan of water to the boil. Add the sago pearls, reduce the heat to medium-low and cook, uncovered, for 30 minutes, or until they become translucent, stirring occasionally to stop the pearls from sticking. Add more boiling water if the sago gets too sticky. Drain in a colander and rinse under running cold water, lightly rubbing the sago to wash away the starch.

2 Divide the sago pearls into 4 to 6 8.5cm/3⅓ inch diameter ramekins. Press down on the sago to level the surface and make compact. Cover with cling film/plastic wrap and chill in the refrigerator for 1 hour.

3 Meanwhile, split the vanilla pod in two, using a small sharp knife, and scrape the seeds into a small saucepan. Add the coconut milk, season generously with salt and place over a medium heat. Slowly bring to the boil, stirring constantly. When bubbles start to form, remove from the heat and strain through a fine sieve into a bowl. Leave to one side to cool.

4 Put the sugar, cocoa powder and 90ml/3fl oz/⅓ cup + 1 tablespoon water into a separate small saucepan over a medium heat. Slowly dissolve the sugar, stirring constantly, until it becomes syrupy. Leave to one side.

5 When the sago is set and chilled, turn the sago out onto individual serving plates. Drizzle over the cocoa sugar syrup and then the coconut milk. Serve slightly chilled.

THAILAND

Thailand is a land abundant with fresh produce, dried spices and fresh aromatic herbs and roots. The Thai are warm and smiling people who firmly believe in how food can bond people. They love to eat and it is because of their passion for food that there are so many amazing dishes to choose from.

Essential ingredients in Thai cooking are fish sauce and dried shrimps, which bring pungency and saltiness to dishes, and are the main components of the often-used flavouring Nam Prik Pao (*see page 235*); bird's eye chillies to add spiciness; tamarind and lime for a delicious sourness; and fresh and fragrant lemongrass, kaffir lime leaves and galangal. Prawn Tom Yum Soup (*see page 151*), sharp in taste with a pleasant chilli kick, is a mouth-watering dish that uses all of these to create perfect harmony.

Other ingredients that are symbolic of Thai cuisine are coconut milk, coriander roots and Thai basil, providing the key flavours in the ubiquitous Thai Green Chicken Curry (*see page 140*), and palm sugar, which delicately balances the sour notes in many Thai dishes, including the superbly refreshing noodle-based dishes Phuket-Style Pad Thai (*see page 148*) and Green Papaya Salad (*see page 155*).

Rice is Thailand's staple food and every meal is based around it. Cellophane or rice noodles are also very popular and they are usually served in a soup or stir-fry – Chiang Mai Curry Noodle Soup (*see page 138*) is an immediately popular example.

CHIANG MAI CURRY NOODLE SOUP

SERVES 4–6
PREPARATION TIME 30 minutes
COOKING TIME 40–45 minutes

250ml/9fl oz/1 cup
  sunflower oil
1 recipe quantity Thai Red
  Curry Spice Paste (*see*
  page 231)
800g/1lb 12oz skinless,
  boneless chicken thighs,
  cut into bite-size pieces
500ml/17fl oz/2 cups
  coconut milk
3 tbsp fish sauce
1 tsp grated palm sugar or
  soft light brown sugar
300g/10½oz dried fine egg
  noodles
200g/7oz dried rice
  vermicelli

TO SERVE
1 handful of coriander/
  cilantro leaves
1 lime, cut into wedges

This curry noodle dish is from north Thailand and takes on influences from its neighbouring country Burma. One of the features of this dish is the deep-fried egg noodles, which add a crunchy texture.

1 Heat 1 tablespoon of the oil in a large saucepan over a medium-high heat. Add the spice paste and cook gently, stirring occasionally, for 10–15 minutes until fragrant and the oil starts to rise to the surface. Add the chicken and toss until each piece of chicken is well coated in the paste, then cook, stirring occasionally, for 8–10 minutes until the chicken starts to turn golden brown.

2 Add half of the coconut milk and gently boil for 5–7 minutes until the coconut milk starts to thicken, then add the remaining coconut milk and 1 litre/35fl oz/4 cups water. Push the chicken around the pan until well coated with the sauce. Add the fish sauce and sugar and cook for a further 10 minutes, or until the chicken is cooked through.

3 Meanwhile, heat the remaining oil in a deep, heavy-based saucepan to 170°C/325°F or until a small piece of bread turns brown in 20 seconds. Take 50g/1¾oz of the egg noodles and separate the strands. Fry the strands in small batches until golden brown all round and leave to one side.

4 Prepare a large bowl of ice-cold water and place it next to the hob/stovetop. Fill a large saucepan with plenty of water and bring to the boil, then add the remaining egg noodles and cook for 3–4 minutes. Using a noodle skimmer or kitchen tongs, remove the noodles from the water and plunge for a few seconds into the cold water, meanwhile bringing the water in the pan back to the boil. Return the noodles to the pan for a few seconds to warm through, then drain and divide the noodles into bowls. Use the same process to cook the dried vermicelli, except cook for 2–3 minutes.

5 Add the chicken pieces and hot curry broth. Top with the fried egg noodles, sprinkle over the coriander and serve with lime wedges on the side.

139

thai green chicken curry

My introduction to Thai Green Chicken Curry was as a teenager, and as my interest in this fresh-flavoured curry grew I learned to make green curry paste from scratch, and have discovered that the most important ingredient is coriander root because of its intense flavour. If you cannot find coriander root, use the coriander leaves and stalks instead.

SERVES **4**
PREPARATION TIME **30 minutes**
COOKING TIME **40 minutes**

500g/1lb 2oz chicken
 drumsticks or skinless
 chicken thighs
2 tsp sunflower oil
1 recipe quantity Thai Green
 Curry Spice Paste (*see
 page 231*)
3 kaffir lime leaves
200ml/7fl oz/scant 1 cup
 thick coconut milk
100g/3½oz pea aubergines/
 eggplants
6 apple aubergines/
 eggplants, cut in half
2 tbsp fish sauce
50g/1¾oz Thai basil leaves

TO SERVE
1 recipe quantity Boiled
 Long-Grain Rice (*see page
 237 – optional*)

1 If using chicken drumsticks, rinse them under running cold water and pat dry with paper towels. Remove the skin and then, using a sharp cleaver or large chef's knife, cut each drumstick into 2 pieces through the bone. Remove the knuckles with a pair of kitchen scissors.

2 Heat the oil in a large saucepan over a medium-high heat. Add the spice paste and cook gently, stirring occasionally, for 10–15 minutes, until fragrant and the oil starts to rise to the surface. Add the kaffir lime leaves and chicken pieces and toss the chicken until well coated with the paste, then cook, stirring occasionally, for 5–6 minutes until starting to turn golden brown.

3 Add the coconut milk to the pan and bring to the boil, then add the pea and apple aubergines and fish sauce. Reduce the heat to low and simmer for 20–25 minutes until the sauce starts to thicken, the chicken is cooked through and the aubergines are soft. Carefully scoop off any oil as it forms on the surface. Stir in the Thai basil and serve warm with boiled rice, if you like.

THAI-STYLE STEAMED FISH WITH LIME, GARLIC & CHILLI

SERVES **4**
PREPARATION TIME **15 minutes**
COOKING TIME **15–20 minutes**

1 x 800g/1lb 12oz whole sea bream, sea bass, grey mullet, barramundi or any other white-fleshed fish, scaled and gutted by your fishmonger
3 lemongrass stalks, crushed
½ tsp sea salt
1½ tbsp grated palm sugar
8 garlic cloves, finely chopped
4–5 red bird's eye chillies, deseeded and chopped
55ml/1¾fl oz/scant ¼ cup fish sauce
80ml/2½fl oz/⅓ cup lime juice
1 big handful of coriander/cilantro leaves, chopped
a few slices of lime

TO SERVE
1 recipe quantity Boiled Long-Grain Rice (*see page 237*)

Hot, spicy, salty and sour! This is right up my street and a dish that I can eat every day with boiled white rice. Simple yet bursting with flavours. For those who like it sour, adding more lime juice will make it even more appetizing.

1 Rinse the fish inside and out under running cold water and pat dry with paper towels. Using a sharp knife, make three diagonal slits on both sides of the fish. Cut off the top of the lemongrass stalks, then stuff into the cavity of the fish. Season the fish with the salt and place on a heatproof plate.

2 Place several round cookie cutters or a wire cooling rack with legs at least 2.5cm/1in tall inside a wok. Leaving a minimum gap of 1cm/½in below this 'steamer', add water to the wok and bring to the boil over a medium-high heat. Set the heatproof plate with the fish on the rack and steam, covered, for 10–15 minutes, or until the flesh separates from the bone easily and looks opaque when a fork is inserted. Keep an eye on the level of the water, adding more boiling water, if necessary.

3 Meanwhile, pour 200ml/7fl oz/scant 1 cup of water into a saucepan, place over a medium heat and bring it to the boil, then remove from the heat. Tip in the palm sugar and mix until it is dissolved. Add in the garlic, bird's eye chillies, fish sauce and lime juice. Mix well. Adjust the sweetness or saltiness or sourness by adding more sugar, fish sauce and lime juice as required.

4 Once the fish is fully steamed, discard the lemongrass and liquid. Transfer the fish to a serving dish with a rim and gently pour over the sauce mixture. Sprinkle over the chopped coriander leaves and garnish with lime slices. Serve immediately with boiled rice.

tHAI ROASt CHICKEN

This Thai-style roast chicken, Gai Yaang, is a very popular Thai street food. During my first visit to southern Thailand, when I was young, I remember visiting one particular market, and still remember the aromas of the Gai Yaang. Traditionally, this dish is cooked over a charcoal grill and is served with rice or Green Papaya Salad (*see page 155*).

SERVES **4**
PREPARATION TIME **30 minutes, plus minimum 6 hours 30 minutes marinating and resting time**
COOKING TIME **45 minutes to 1 hour**

1 x 1.5kg/3lb 5oz whole chicken
1 tbsp sea salt
1 recipe quantity Thai Roast Chicken Spice Paste (*see page 231*)
2 tbsp fish sauce
1 tbsp clear honey

TO SERVE
Green Papaya Salad (*see page 155*)

1 Remove the neck, gizzards and fat from inside the chicken. Rinse the chicken thoroughly inside and out under running cold water. Lightly rub the salt onto the skin, then rinse the chicken again and pat dry with paper towels. To spatchcock the chicken, place it breast-side down on a chopping/cutting board and then, using a pair of kitchen scissors, cut off the tail and cut along each side of the backbone, discarding the bone. Turn the chicken over and press down on the breast to slightly flatten the chicken.

2 Mix together the spice paste, fish sauce and honey in a large bowl, then add the chicken and thoroughly coat all round with the mixture. Transfer to a plate, cover with cling film/plastic wrap and leave to marinate in the refrigerator for 6 hours or, for and even better flavour, overnight.

3 Remove the chicken from the refrigerator and leave to stand at room temperature for 30 minutes before cooking. Preheat the oven to 180°C/350°F/Gas 4. Put the chicken on a baking sheet and bake for 45 minutes–1 hour until golden and cooked through. When the tip of a sharp knife is inserted into the thickest part of the meat, the juices should run clear. Remove from the oven and leave to rest for 5 minutes.

4 To serve, cut the chicken in half through the breast. Take one side of the chicken and, using a sharp knife, cut through the bone to remove the thigh and drumstick whole. Cut through the joint to remove the wing, then cut the breast into 4 chunky pieces. Repeat the same steps to cut up the other half of the chicken. Serve hot with the Green Papaya Salad.

SERVES **4**
PREPARATION TIME **20 minutes**
COOKING TIME **20 minutes**

100g/3½oz/⅔ cup pine nuts
2 tbsp sunflower oil
500g/1lb 2oz boneless,
   skinless chicken breasts, cut
   into bite-size pieces
1 red onion, cut into wedges
4 garlic cloves, finely chopped
4 dried chillies, deseeded,
   soaked and chopped
2 tsp nam prik pao (*see page
   235*)
2 tsp fish sauce
1 tsp clear honey
2 spring onions/scallions, cut
   into 5cm/2in lengths
1 recipe quantity Boiled
   Long-Grain Rice, to serve
   (*see page 237*)

SPICY CHICKEN & PINE NUT STIR-FRY

1 Heat a frying pan over a medium-high heat, then add the pine nuts and dry-roast until fragrant and starting to brown. Leave to one side.
2 Add 1 tablespoon of the oil to the frying pan and when the oil is hot, add the chicken pieces and stir-fry for 1–2 minutes until sealed. Using a slotted spoon, remove the chicken from the pan, drain on paper towels and leave to one side.
3 Clean the pan, then heat the remaining tablespoon of oil over a medium-high heat. Add the onion, garlic and dried chillies and stir-fry for 2–3 minutes until the onion starts to soften. Add the nam prik pao and stir-fry for 1 minute, then toss through the seared chicken and pine nuts. Add the fish sauce and honey and cook, stirring occasionally, for about 6 minutes, or until the chicken is golden and cooked through. Add in the spring onions and stir-fry for 1 minute before serving immediately with boiled rice.

SERVES **4**
PREPARATION TIME **25 minutes**
COOKING TIME **20 minutes**

1 tbsp sunflower oil
5 garlic cloves, finely chopped
500g/1lb 2oz minced/ground
   pork
2 tsp nam prik pao (*see page 235*)
1 tsp oyster sauce
2 tsp fish sauce
1 tsp grated palm sugar or soft
   light brown sugar
1 handful of Thai basil leaves
1 recipe quantity Boiled
   Long-Grain Rice, to serve
   (*see page 237*)

CHILLI & THAI BASIL PORK

1 Heat the oil in a wok over a medium-high heat. Add the garlic and stir-fry for 1–2 minutes until fragrant. Tip in the pork, break up the lumps and cook, stirring occasionally, for 5 minutes.
2 Stir in the nam prik pao, oyster sauce, fish sauce and sugar and add 100ml/3½fl oz/generous ⅓ cup water. Bring to the boil, then reduce the heat to medium and cook, stirring occasionally, for 4–5 minutes until the pork is cooked. Add the Thai basil leaves, toss for a few seconds and serve immediately with boiled rice.

THAI FRIED RICE WITH PORK & MANGO SALAD

SERVES 4–6
PREPARATION TIME 30 minutes, plus 5–10 minutes soaking time and cooking and chilling the rice
COOKING TIME 20 minutes

25g/1oz dried shrimps
2 tbsp sunflower oil
250g/9oz minced/ground pork
3 garlic cloves, finely chopped
1 tbsp chopped coriander/cilantro stems and leaves
1 recipe quantity Boiled Long-Grain Rice, cooked and chilled for 12 hours or overnight (*see page 237*)
1 tbsp nam prik pao (*see page 235*)
2 tbsp fish sauce
1 tbsp dark soy sauce
Sambal (*see page 236*), to serve

MANGO SALAD
250g/9oz green mango
2 shallots, thinly sliced
2 red bird's eye chillies, deseeded and chopped
2 tbsp fish sauce
2 tbsp lime juice
2 tbsp grated palm sugar or soft light brown sugar
1 handful of mint leaves, roughly chopped
1 handful of coriander/cilantro leaves, roughly chopped

I discovered this recipe by accident at a roadside stall run by a Malay-Thai family. This dish was one of their specialities – Thai-style fried rice topped with well-flavoured pork and mango salad served with a small portion of sambal. The taste combination is amazing, and this dish is comfort food at its best. Mix everything together and tuck in.

1 Put the dried shrimps in a small bowl, cover with water and leave to soak for 5–10 minutes. Drain and squeeze out any excess water, pat dry with paper towels and then roughly chop and leave to one side.

2 Meanwhile, to make the mango salad, peel the green mango with a potato peeler, then either use a mandoline or zigzag peeler to shred the flesh, leaving behind the flesh nearest the seed. Put the shredded mango in a bowl of cold salted water for 1–2 minutes to draw out the acidity. Drain, pat dry with paper towels and transfer to a bowl.

3 Put the shallots and chillies in a mortar and lightly bruise them using a pestle. Alternatively, place on a chopping/cutting board and bruise with the flat of a knife blade. Put the minced shallots and chillies in a food processor with the fish sauce, lime juice and sugar and blend until the sugar is dissolved. Pour the mixture over the shredded mango, add the mint and coriander and toss to mix through. Set aside.

4 Heat 1 tablespoon of the oil in a frying pan over a high heat. Tip in the pork, break up the lumps and stir-fry for 2 minutes. Stir in the garlic and coriander and cook, stirring occasionally, for 4–5 minutes until the pork is cooked through. Remove from the heat and keep warm.

5 Heat the remaining tablespoon of oil in a wok or frying pan over a high heat until smoking hot. Add the prepared shrimps and cook for 1–2 minutes until fragrant. Tip in the cooked rice, break up any lumps and stir-fry for 2–3 minutes. Add the nam prik pao, fish sauce and soy sauce and stir to combine, and cook for a further 4–5 minutes until heated through. Divide the fried rice onto plates, spoon the pork on top and then sprinkle over the mango salad. Serve hot with the mango salad and sambal.

BEEF PANANG CURRY

Rich, sweet and creamy with a dark red undertone, this is a lovely comfort dish. In comparison to the ever famous green curry, Panang Curry gives a different dimension with the touch of roasted peanuts. Beef is the popular type of meat to use; however, pork or chicken can also be used and are delicious.

SERVES **4**
PREPARATION TIME **15 minutes**
COOKING TIME **35–45 minutes**

1 x 500g/1lb 2oz beef fillet
400ml/14fl oz/generous 1½ cups coconut milk
1 recipe quantity Panang Curry Spice Paste (*see page 229*)
2 kaffir lime leaves, thinly sliced
50g/1¾oz/⅓ cup skinless raw peanuts
2 tbsp fish sauce
1 tbsp clear honey

TO SERVE
Thai basil leaves
1 recipe quantity Boiled Long-Grain Rice (*see page 237*)

1 Put the beef fillet on a chopping/cutting board and then, using a sharp knife, cut against the grain into 5mm/¼in slices and leave to one side.

2 Pour half of the coconut milk into a large saucepan over a medium-high heat and bring to a gentle boil. Add the spice paste and cook, stirring occasionally, for 4–5 minutes until the paste starts to thicken. Add the remaining coconut milk and kaffir lime leaves and cook, stirring occasionally, for a further 3–4 minutes until fragrant and the oil starts to rise to the surface.

3 Meanwhile, heat a frying pan over a medium-high heat, then add the peanuts and dry-roast until fragrant and starting to brown. Remove from the heat and roughly chop.

4 Tip the beef slices into the saucepan and push around until well coated with the sauce. Cook for a further 4–5 minutes, then stir in the fish sauce and honey. Reduce the heat to low and simmer, covered, for 10–15 minutes until the meat is tender. Five minutes before the end of cooking, stir in the roasted peanuts. Sprinkle over the Thai basil and serve immediately with boiled rice.

CLAYPOT PRAWNS & NOODLES

SERVES 4
PREPARATION TIME 20 minutes
COOKING TIME 20–25 minutes

8 raw, unpeeled large king
  prawns/jumbo shrimp/
  jumbo shrimp
2 tbsp sunflower oil
3 garlic cloves, finely
  chopped
2cm/¾in piece of fresh
  ginger, peeled and cut into
  thin matchsticks
200g/7oz dried glass
  noodles, such as bean
  thread vermicelli, soaked in
  warm water for 5 minutes
1 small handful of coriander/
  cilantro, roughly chopped

SAUCE
1 tbsp sesame oil
½ tsp ground white pepper
2 tbsp oyster sauce
2 tbsp Chinese cooking wine
1½ tbsp fish sauce
1½ tbsp granulated sugar
3 tsp dark soy sauce

This dish is a meal on its own. Fresh prawns can be substituted with other types of protein, such as crab, if you like. The use of a claypot is very common in Asia and this way of cooking helps to capture the flavours of all the different ingredients and keeps the prawns tender and moist.

1 Using a pair of kitchen scissors, trim from from each prawn/shrimp the feelers, rostrum, legs and the sharp end of the tail. Make a slit along the back of each prawn with a sharp knife and pull out the black vein with the tip of the knife or your fingers. Rinse the prawns under running cold water and pat dry with paper towels. Put to one side.

2 To make the sauce, put all the ingredients in a small bowl and gently whisk until combined. Leave to one side.

3 Heat the sunflower oil in a medium-large claypot or a heatproof casserole dish over a medium-high heat. Add the garlic and ginger and stir-fry for 1 minute, or until fragrant. Add 200ml/7fl oz/scant 1 cup of water and the sauce and mix well. Bring to the boil for about 2 minutes, then tip in the glass noodles.

4 Arrange the prawns on top of the noodles and reduce the heat to medium-low, cover with the lid and cook for a further 10 minutes, or until the prawns and glass noodles are fully cooked. The noodles should be moist, so add more water if needed. Remove from the heat, sprinkle over the chopped coriander and serve hot.

PHUKET-STYLE PAD THAI

Pad Thai is one of Thailand's much-loved national dishes that is sold from street carts on most street corners. This Phuket-Style Pad Thai is unique, as it is served on an omelette instead of mixing the shredded omelette into the noodles.

SERVES **4**
PREPARATION TIME **20 minutes**
COOKING TIME **about**
30 minutes, plus cooking the rice sticks

2 tbsp sunflower oil, plus extra for frying, if needed
5 eggs, beaten
50g/1¾oz/⅓ cup skinless raw peanuts
60g/2¼oz firm tofu, cut into strips
3 garlic cloves, finely chopped
250g/9oz raw, peeled large king prawns/jumbo shrimp, deveined (*see page 241*)
3 tbsp fish sauce
1 tbsp dark soy sauce
2 tsp nam prik pao (*see page 235*)
2 tbsp lime juice
2 tsp grated palm sugar or soft light brown sugar
300g/10½oz cooked 5mm/¼in rice sticks (*see page 238*)
150g/5½oz/1¼ cups bean sprouts
3 spring onions/scallions or Chinese chives, cut lengthways into 5cm/2in pieces
1 handful of coriander/cilantro leaves, to serve

1 Heat 1 tablespoon of the oil in a 20cm/8in frying pan over a medium heat. Pour one-quarter of the beaten eggs into the pan and swirl around to evenly coat the base. Cook for 2–3 minutes until the surface starts to set. Using a spatula, turn the omelette over and cook on the other side for 2–3 minutes until cooked through. Slide the omelette onto a plate, then repeat with the remaining egg to make 4 omelette s, adding more oil to the pan if necessary.

2 Meanwhile, heat a frying pan over a medium-high heat, then add the peanuts and dry-roast until fragrant and starting to brown. Remove from the heat and roughly grind the peanuts in a food processor or blender – you want a fine powder with some chunky bits.

3 Heat the remaining 1 tablespoon of oil in a wok or large frying pan over a medium-high heat. Add the tofu and stir-fry for 8–10 minutes until lightly golden brown, then add the garlic and stir-fry for 1–2 minutes until fragrant. Tip in the prawns and cook, stirring occasionally, for 3–4 minutes until they turn pink and are cooked through. Meanwhile, mix the fish sauce, soy sauce, nam prik pao, lime juice and sugar in a small bowl until the sugar is dissolved.

4 Drain the cooked rice sticks, refresh under running cold water and pat dry with paper towels. Add the sticks to the wok with the prawns and toss until well combined, then pour over the sauce mixture. Push the ingredients around the pan until well combined, then add 3–4 tablespoons water and stir-fry for 2–3 minutes. Toss through the bean sprouts and spring onions and cook for 1 minute, or until heated through.

5 Put an omelette on each dish, then divide the Pad Thai over the omelettes and sprinkle over the roasted peanuts and coriander. Serve hot.

PRAWN tom yum SOUP

SERVES 4–6
PREPARATION TIME **30 minutes,**
plus making the stock
COOKING TIME **20 minutes**

16 raw, unpeeled large king
prawns/jumbo shrimp
½ recipe quantity Chicken
Stock (*see page 232*)
3 lemongrass stalks, outer
leaves and stalk ends
removed, crushed and cut
into 5cm/2in pieces
6 kaffir lime leaves, bruised
5 shallots, peeled and
crushed
6–8 red bird's eye chillies,
whole and slightly bruised
2cm/¾in piece of fresh
ginger or galangal, peeled
and sliced
200g/7oz oyster mushrooms
or button mushrooms
2 tbsp nam prik pao (*see
page 235*)
2 tbsp fish sauce
7 tbsp lime juice
2 tsp grated palm sugar or
soft light brown sugar
½ tsp sea salt
2 tomatoes, skinned and cut
into quarters (*see page
242*)
1 handful of coriander/
cilantro leaves, to serve

Hot, sour, sweet and salty – these words sum up perfectly this irresistible bowl of Tom Yum Goong. Its distinct flavours are the result of infusing the stock with ginger or galangal as well as fresh lemongrass and kaffir lime leaves, which give a zesty hint of citrus. As an alternative, use chicken thighs or breast instead of the prawns.

1 Using a pair of kitchen scissors, trim from each prawn the feelers, rostrum, legs and the sharp end of the tail. Make a slit along the back of the prawn with a sharp knife and pull out the black vein with the tip of the knife or your fingers. Rinse the prawns under running cold water and pat dry with paper towels.

2 Pour the chicken stock into a large saucepan and bring to the boil over a medium-high heat. Add the lemongrass, kaffir lime leaves, shallots, chillies and ginger and cook for 5 minutes, or until fragrant. Add the prawns to the pan, cover and bring back to the boil. Reduce the heat to low and cook for 5–7 minutes until the prawns turn pink and are cooked through.

3 Add the mushrooms to the pan and cook for 2 minutes, then stir in the nam prik pao, fish sauce, lime juice, sugar and salt. The broth should taste sour, slightly salty and sweet. Add more lime juice, if you like. Tip in the tomatoes, bring back to the boil, then remove the pan from the heat.

4 Discard the lemongrass, kaffir lime leaves, shallots and ginger, and serve immediately with the coriander sprinkled over.

SERVES **4**
PREPARATION TIME **30 minutes**
COOKING TIME **5–7 minutes**

500g/1lb 2oz squid, cut into
 rings and tentacles into
 pieces (*see page 241*)
10 cherry tomatoes, halved
1 handful of coriander/
 cilantro leaves

DRESSING
2 green bird's eye chillies,
 deseeded and finely
 chopped
1 red chilli, deseeded and
 finely chopped
2 tbsp fish sauce
3 tbsp lime juice
1 tbsp grated palm sugar or
 soft light brown sugar

SPICY STEAMED SQUID

1 Combine all the dressing ingredients in a bowl, stirring until the sugar is dissolved. Place the squid on a plate and place in a bamboo or electric steamer and steam the squid for 5–7 minutes until it starts to curl up around the edges and is cooked through.

2 Remove the squid from the steamer and leave to stand at room temperature for 5 minutes, then transfer to a bowl. Toss through the cherry tomatoes and coriander, then pour over the dressing. Serve at room temperature.

SERVES **4**
PREPARATION TIME **15 minutes**
COOKING TIME **10–15 minutes**

1 tbsp sunflower oil
2 garlic cloves, finely
 chopped
200g/7oz raw, peeled large
 king prawns/jumbo shrimp,
 deveined (*see page 241*)
1 tbsp nam prik pao
 (*see page 235*)
400g/14oz water spinach or
 baby leaf spinach
1 tsp fish sauce

PRAWN & WATER SPINACH STIR-FRY

1 Heat the oil in a frying pan over a medium-high heat, then add the garlic and cook for 1–2 minutes until fragrant. Add the prawns and stir-fry for 5 minutes, or until they turn pink and are cooked through, then add the nam prik pao and cook for 1 minute.

2 Add the spinach, toss to combine and then cook for 3–4 minutes if using water spinach, and 1 minute if using baby spinach, or until the spinach starts to wilt. Add the fish sauce and 3 tablespoons water, stirring until well combined. Serve immediately.

GReen PAPAYA SALAD

SERVES **4**
PREPARATION TIME **45 minutes,**
   plus **15–20 minutes**
   soaking time
COOKING TIME **5–10 minutes**

30g/1oz dried shrimps
50g/1¾oz/⅓ cup raw,
   skinless peanuts
400g/14oz firm green
   papaya or green mango
3 garlic cloves, chopped
2 red bird's eye chillies,
   deseeded and chopped
80g/2¾oz green beans or
   Chinese long beans,
   trimmed and cut into
   4cm/1½in pieces
4 tbsp fish sauce
4 tbsp lime juice
2 tbsp grated palm sugar or
   soft light brown sugar
12 cherry tomatoes, halved
sea salt

A wonderfully simple dish with sweet, sour, spicy and slightly salty flavours. If you can't find green papaya, substitute it with green mango, which usually can be found at Chinese supermarkets. Green mango can be a bit sour compared to the milder flavour of green papaya, so you may have to adjust the acidity by adding more palm sugar.

1 Put the dried shrimps in a small bowl, cover with water and leave to soak for 5–10 minutes.

2 Heat a frying pan over a medium-high heat, then add the peanuts and dry-roast until fragrant and starting to brown. Remove from the heat and leave to one side.

3 Peel the green papaya with a potato peeler, then either use a mandoline or zigzag peeler to shred the flesh, leaving behind the flesh nearest the seed. Put the shredded papaya in a bowl of cold salted water for 1–2 minutes to draw out the acidity and firm up the flesh. Drain, pat dry with paper towels and transfer to a bowl.

4 Squeeze out any excess water from the dried shrimps and pat dry with paper towels. Roughly chop into chunky pieces and put in a separate bowl.

5 Put the garlic and chillies in a large bowl and bruise with a pestle or the end of a rolling pin until they are almost mashed. Add the green beans, little by little, and bruise until all the beans start splitting. Add the prepared shrimps and peanuts and continue to pound and bruise until the shrimps and peanuts are roughly crushed and all the ingredients are well mixed.

6 Combine the fish sauce, lime juice and sugar in a small bowl until the sugar is dissolved. Slowly add the sauce to the shrimp and bean mixture, blending as you pour.

7 When everything is well pounded and mixed, slowly add the shredded papaya, mixing and lightly pounding between each addition. Finally, add the cherry tomatoes, toss well and serve immediately.

STICKY COCONUT RICE WITH CARAMELIZED MANGO

A popular Thai dessert with a silky smooth texture and a great flavour. For a truly authentic dish, try to get Thai mangoes, *nam dok mai*, which are ripened on the tree so are much sweeter and tastier. Here I've given this dish an added dimension by caramelizing the mangoes.

SERVES 4
PREPARATION TIME 15 minutes, plus 1 hour 40 minutes soaking and resting time
COOKING TIME 35–40 minutes

300g/10½oz/1½ cups glutinous rice
350ml/12fl oz/scant 1½ cups coconut milk
4 tbsp granulated sugar
¼ tsp fine sea salt
2 ripe mangoes
60g/2¼oz/heaped ¼ cup caster/superfine sugar

1 Put the rice in a bowl, cover with cold water and soak for about 1 hour. Drain through a fine sieve and leave to stand for 15 minutes. Line a bamboo or electric steamer with muslin/cheesecloth and spread the soaked rice over the muslin. Steam the rice for about 20 minutes, or until it becomes translucent and is soft all the way through. Turn off the heat and let the rice sit in the steamer for about a further 5 minutes.

2 Meanwhile, pour the coconut milk into a saucepan over a medium heat and slowly bring to the boil. Remove from the heat, add the granulated sugar and salt and stir until the sugar is dissolved. Leave to one side.

3 Remove the rice in the muslin from the steamer and tip into a bowl. Pour 300ml/10½fl oz/scant 1¼ cups of the sugared coconut milk over the rice and mix well. Cover with cling film/plastic wrap and leave to stand for about 25 minutes to allow the rice to absorb the coconut milk.

4 Meanwhile, peel the mangoes with a potato peeler. Taking one mango, slice off the stem end to create a flat surface, then, holding the mango upright and using a sharp knife, slice downwards from top to bottom to cut off one side of the mango. As you slice down, use the flat edge of the seed as your guide. Slice off the other side, then repeat with the second mango. Cut the mango flesh into 1.5cm/⅝in strips lengthways.

5 Mix together the caster sugar and 55ml/1¾fl oz/scant ¼ cup water in a large saucepan over a medium-high heat, stirring until the sugar dissolves. Bring to a gentle boil, reduce the heat to medium and simmer, without stirring, for 3–4 minutes until the mixture thickens and turns light brown. Reduce the heat to medium-low, add the mangoes and cook for about 5 minutes.

6 Divide the sticky rice onto individual dessert plates.
Top with the caramelized mango strips and pour over
the remaining sugared coconut milk.
Serve at room temperature.

CAMBODIA & VIETNAM

Fresh, sweet, sour and salty with a gentle spiciness; this sums up Cambodian cuisine, and the taste of each dish mirrors the country itself: warm, beautiful and full of character and flavour.

Cambodian food shares many similarities with that of its neighbours – Laos, Thailand and Vietnam. From a simple dish of Cambodian Beef Stir-Fry with Chilli Sauce (*see page 168*), with a superb balance of citrus, saltiness and sweetness to a flavoursome bowl of Khmer Yellow Chicken Curry (*see page 162*), which uses many of the essential ingredients of all these cuisines, including lemongrass, lime leaves, coriander, chillies, coconut milk, shrimp paste and galangal.

Rice noodles and rice are the two food staples in neighbouring Vietnam, where the food is typically light and refreshing – perfect for the hot and humid climate. Grilled Beef Salad (*see page 181*), which is made with a slightly pungent-tasting fish sauce and a generous amount of the fresh and fragrant herbs basil and coriander, is a perfect example of this light and tasty cuisine. Vietnamese Chicken Noodle Soup (*see page 160*) is the national dish and uses the spices star anise, black pepper and cloves to give fragrance and subtle depth, something else that is common to many Vietnamese dishes.

VIETNAMESE CHICKEN NOODLE SOUP

SERVES **4–6**
PREPARATION TIME **10 minutes**
COOKING TIME **2 hours 15 minutes**

1 x 2kg/4lb 8oz whole chicken
1 tsp sea salt
½ tsp black peppercorns
2 star anise
3 cloves
2 whole onions and 1 onion, finely sliced
8cm/3¼in piece of fresh ginger, peeled and finely chopped
4 garlic cloves, unpeeled
3 tbsp fish sauce
1 tbsp granulated sugar
150g/5½oz/1¼ cups bean sprouts
250g/9oz cooked 3mm/⅛in or 5mm/¼in rice sticks (*see page 238*)

TO SERVE
10 sprigs Thai basil
1 small handful of tarragon leaves, roughly chopped
1 small handful of coriander/cilantro leaves
2 red chillies, sliced
1 lime, cut into wedges

During my recent trip to Vietnam, I went in search of a real pho (pronounced fuh) experience. This noodle soup, known as Pho Ga, is a truly satisfying and complete meal. Because it is simmered at a very low heat, with the surface barely moving, the stock is really clear with no cloudiness. The gentle simmering also means the spices slowly infuse the stock, producing a really rich and deep flavour.

1 Rinse the chicken thoroughly inside and out under running cold water. Lightly rub the salt on the skin, then rinse the chicken again and pat dry inside and out with paper towels. Put the chicken, breast-side down, in a large saucepan. Put the peppercorns, star anise and cloves in a spice bag or secure in a piece of muslin/cheesecloth and add to the saucepan with the chicken.

2 In a frying pan over a medium-high heat, dry-fry the 2 whole onions, ginger and garlic until slightly charred all around, then put in the saucepan with the chicken.

3 Pour 3 litres/105fl oz/12 cups cold water over the chicken and bring to the boil. Reduce the heat to low and simmer, covered, for about 1 hour, skimming off any scum from the surface as required. After 25 minutes, using kitchen tongs, turn the chicken breast-side up and continue to cook until the end of the cooking time. When the tip of a sharp knife is inserted into the thickest part of the meat the juices should run clear.

4 Remove the chicken from the stock, rinse under running cold water and rest for 10 minutes, or until cool enough to handle. Cut the meat away from the legs and remove the breast meat from the bone in 2 whole pieces. Return the bones to the stock and continue to simmer, covered, for a further 1 hour. Shred or slice the meat, removing the skin and any small bones. Cover with cling film/plastic wrap to keep moist and leave to one side.

5 Take the stock off the heat and remove and discard all the solid ingredients. Leave to cool and then strain over a large bowl through a sieve lined with muslin. Give the saucepan a rinse and pour the stock back in. Bring to a gentle boil over a medium-high heat, add

the fish sauce and sugar, stirring until the sugar is dissolved, then reduce the heat to low and leave gently simmering.

6 Meanwhile, bring a saucepan of water to the boil and blanch the bean sprouts for about 20 seconds. Divide the warm, cooked rice sticks into deep soup bowls, then top with the blanched bean sprouts. Add the shredded chicken and sprinkle over the sliced onion.

7 Meanwhile, bring the stock to a vigorous boil and put the sprigs of Thai basil, the tarragon, coriander, chillies and lime on a plate. Ladle the stock into the bowls and serve immediately with the accompaniments on the side.

KHMER YELLOW CHICKEN CURRY

SERVES 4
PREPARATION TIME 30 minutes
COOKING TIME 30–40 minutes

2 tbsp sunflower oil
1 small onion, roughly chopped
1 recipe quantity Khmer Yellow Curry Spice Paste (*see page 228*)
600g/1lb 5oz boneless, skinless chicken thighs, cut into bite-size pieces
2 kaffir lime leaves
1 carrot, cut into bite-size pieces
400ml/14fl oz/generous 1½ cups coconut milk
2 tbsp fish sauce
1 tbsp grated palm sugar or soft light brown sugar
150g/5½oz green beans, cut lengthways into 5cm/2in pieces

TO SERVE
1 recipe quantity Boiled Long-Grain Rice (*see page 237*)

Spice pastes, *kroeung*, are very important in Khmer cooking, and are regularly used in stir-fries, soups and stews. There are three distinct types of spice pastes – yellow, green and red – and it is the dominant spice used to make the paste that defines its colour. In yellow kroeung it is turmeric; green chilli gives green kroeung its colour; and red chillies produce the bright red colour of red kroeung.

1 Heat the oil in a large frying pan over a medium-high heat. Add the onion and cook for 2–3 minutes until soft and translucent, stirring occasionally. Add the spice paste and cook gently, stirring occasionally, for 10–15 minutes until fragrant and the oil starts to rise to the surface.

2 Tip in the chicken pieces and add the kaffir lime leaves, then push the chicken pieces around the pan until they are well coated with the spice paste. Cook for a further 4–5 minutes, then add the carrots and cook for another 2–3 minutes.

3 Pour the coconut milk into the pan and bring to the boil, then add the fish sauce and sugar and stir until the sugar is dissolved. Tip in the green beans and combine with the other ingredients. Reduce the heat to low and simmer for 10–15 minutes until the sauce starts to thicken and the chicken is cooked through. Serve immediately with boiled rice.

Vietnamese-style CHICKen & PORK PâTé BAGUette

MAKES **4**
PREPARATION TIME **1 hour, plus 2 hours 15 minutes marinating and pickling time and 24–36 hours resting time**
COOKING TIME **45 minutes to 1 hour**

4 sandwich-size baguettes, sliced in half lengthways
1 small cucumber, quartered lengthways, deseeded and cut into matchsticks
chilli sauce, to taste (optional)
2 small handfuls of coriander/cilantro leaves

PÂTÉ
250g/9oz chicken livers
30g/1oz butter
3 shallots, chopped
3 garlic cloves, chopped
1cm/½in piece of fresh ginger, peeled and chopped
250g/9oz pork loin, cubed
1 tsp five-spice powder
4½ tsp fish sauce
¼ tsp sea salt
1 egg, beaten
2 bay leaves

PICKLED CARROT & DAIKON
200g/7oz carrots, grated
200g/7oz daikon, grated
½ tbsp sea salt
3 tbsp clear honey
125ml/4fl oz/½ cup rice vinegar

1 To make the pâté, cut the chicken livers in half and trim off any fibrous tissues. Rinse under running cold water and pat dry with paper towels.

2 Melt the butter in a frying pan over a medium heat, then add the shallots, garlic and ginger. Cook for 2 minutes, or until fragrant and softened, then transfer to a food processor. Add the pork loin and chicken livers and blend to a rough paste.

3 Transfer the paste to a bowl, add the five-spice powder, fish sauce, salt and egg and stir until well combined. Cover with cling film/plastic wrap and leave to marinate in the refrigerator for about 2 hours.

4 To prepare the pickled vegetables, put the shredded carrots and daikon in a bowl, rub in the salt and leave to stand for 5 minutes. Squeeze out as much moisture as possible, then pat dry with paper towels. Return the vegetables to the bowl, mix in the honey and pour in the rice vinegar. Leave to stand at room temperature for at least 1 hour.

5 Remove the marinated pork and chicken liver pâté from the refrigerator and spoon the mixture into an 18 x 14cm/7 x 5½in baking dish. Level the surface and arrange the bay leaves on top. Leave to stand at room temperature for 15 minutes. Meanwhile, preheat the oven to 180°C/350°F/Gas 4.

6 Cover the baking dish tightly with foil and transfer to a large roasting pan. Pour in enough boiling water to come two-thirds of the way up the baking dish, place the roasting pan in the oven and bake for 45 minutes–1 hour, or until the tip of a sharp, fine-bladed knife inserted into the centre of the pâté comes out clean.

7 Remove the foil and bay leaves from the pâté. Leave to cool at room temperature, then cover with cling film/plastic wrap and refrigerate for 24–36 hours. When ready to serve, turn the pâté out onto a chopping/cutting board and cut into 1cm/½in slices.

8 Spread 2 generous slices of pâté over each baguette, then top with the cucumber strips and pickled carrot and daikon. Spoon over the chilli sauce, if using, and sprinkle over the coriander and serve. Any unused pickled vegetables can be stored in a jar in the refrigerator for up to 1 month.

PHNOM PENH NOODLE SOUP

SERVES 4–6

PREPARATION TIME **20 minutes, plus making the stock and soaking and cooking the noodles**

COOKING TIME **about 1 hour, plus cooking the noodles**

1 recipe quantity Pork Stock (*see page 232*)

1 onion

½ tsp coriander seeds

2 cloves

¼ tsp Sichuan peppercorns

250g/9oz minced/ground pork

1 spring onion/scallion, finely chopped

1 tbsp sunflower oil

200g/7oz raw, peeled king prawns/jumbo shrimp, deveined (*see page 241*)

150g/5½oz/1¼ cups bean sprouts

250g/9oz cooked thick rice noodles (*see page 238*)

2 tbsp fish sauce

2 tsp sugar

sea salt and freshly ground black pepper

TO SERVE

1 small handful of coriander leaves

2 tbsp Fried Shallots (*see page 235*)

1 lime, cut into wedges

bean sprouts

1 Pour the pork stock into a saucepan and bring to the boil over a high heat. Reduce the heat to low and simmer. Meanwhile, dry-fry the whole onion in a frying pan over a medium-high heat until the outer layer is slightly charred all round. Add the charred onion to the simmering stock. Put the coriander seeds, cloves and Sichuan peppercorns in a spice bag or secure in a piece of muslin/cheesecloth and add into the stock. Continue to simmer, covered, for 45 minutes.

2 Put the pork in a bowl and season with salt and pepper. Tip into a food processor and blend to a smooth paste. Put the pork back into the bowl, add the spring onion and mix until well combined. Using a teaspoon or melon baller, scoop up the paste and shape into chestnut-size balls and arrange on a plate – they don't need to be perfectly round. Repeat until all the pork paste is used. Cover with cling film/plastic wrap and leave to one side.

3 Heat the oil in a large frying pan over a medium-high heat. Add the prawns and stir-fry for 3–4 minutes until they turn pink and are cooked through. Transfer to a plate and leave to one side.

4 Bring a saucepan of water to the boil and blanch the bean sprouts for about 20 seconds. Divide the warm, cooked noodles into deep soup bowls, then top with the blanched bean sprouts.

5 Bring the stock back to the boil, then add the pork balls and cook for 4–5 minutes until they are cooked through and float to the surface. Divide the pork balls into the bowls of noodles and add the cooked prawns.

6 Add the fish sauce, a generous pinch of salt and the sugar to the pork stock and bring to a vigorous boil. Ladle the stock into the bowls, then sprinkle over the coriander and fried shallots. Serve immediately with the lime wedges and extra bean sprouts on the side.

CAMBODIAN BEEF STIR-FRY WITH CHILLI SAUCE

This dish was brought to Cambodia from Vietnam during the French colonization. The name in Vietnamese, Bo Luc Lac, literally means 'shaking beef', and this recipe is based on a delicious version I ate in Phnom Penh. I've added honey and used dark soy sauce, which make it stand out in flavour.

SERVES 4
PREPARATION TIME 30 minutes, plus minimum 1 hour marinating time
COOKING TIME about 10 minutes

500g/1lb 2oz sirloin, cut into bite-size pieces
5 garlic cloves, finely chopped
½ tsp sea salt
¼ tsp freshly ground black pepper
¼ tsp cinnamon
2 tsp dark soy sauce
2 tbsp sunflower oil
150g/5½oz lettuce leaves, roughly torn
2 tomatoes, sliced
1 small cucumber, deseeded and cut into chunks
1 small red onion, thinly sliced
1 tbsp fish sauce
1 tbsp tomato ketchup
2 tsp honey

CHILLI SAUCE
½ tsp sea salt
¼ tsp freshly ground black pepper
1 small red chilli, deseeded and sliced
juice of 1 lime

TO SERVE
1 recipe quantity Boiled Long-Grain Rice (*see page 237* – optional)

1 To prepare the chilli sauce, mix all the ingredients in a small bowl and leave to one side.

2 Put the sirloin, garlic, salt, black pepper, cinnamon and soy sauce in a large bowl and mix well. Cover with cling film/plastic wrap and leave to marinate in the refrigerator for 1 hour or, for and even better flavour, overnight.

3 Heat the oil in a wok or large frying pan over a high heat until smoking hot. Tip in the beef and marinade and stir-fry for 5–7 minutes until the beef is browned and the liquid has evaporated. Add the fish sauce, tomato ketchup and honey to the wok and push the beef around until well coated. Cook for a further 1 minute, then spoon the beef over the salad, drizzle over the chilli sauce and serve immediately with boiled rice, if you like.

CARAMELIZED SALMON WITH PINEAPPLE

SERVES 4
PREPARATION TIME 45 minutes
COOKING TIME about 25 minutes

4 x 250g/9oz boneless, unskinned salmon steaks (about 2.5–3cm/1–1¼in thick)
1 tbsp sunflower oil
3 garlic cloves, finely chopped
1 small red chilli, deseeded and finely diced
2 tbsp granulated sugar
1 tbsp clear honey
¼ tsp freshly ground black pepper
4 tbsp fish sauce
2 tsp dark soy sauce
200g/7oz pineapple, peeled, cored and cut into bite-size pieces

TO SERVE
1 recipe quantity Boiled Long-Grain Rice (*see page 237* – optional)

The combination of sweetness and saltiness with a touch of chilli in this dish goes well with just about any fish, but it is particularly good with the buttery richness of salmon. If you want to try it with a white-fleshed fish, I suggest either haddock or monkfish. Fish steaks work better than fillets, which easily break into pieces.

1 For each salmon steak, using the tip of a small, sharp knife, carefully slice the skin away from the flesh from the bottom two sides of the steaks, leaving it intact on the upper halves. Fold the skinned pieces of fish into the centre of the steak to create a circular shape, then wrap the loose pieces of skin around the outside. Secure in place with kitchen string/twine. This is known as a fish noisette.

2 Heat the oil in a frying pan over a medium-high heat. Add the garlic and chilli and stir-fry for 1–2 minutes until fragrant. Add the sugar, honey, pepper, fish sauce and soy sauce and stir until the sugar is dissolved. Simmer, stirring constantly, for 2 minutes, or until the sauce starts to caramelize.

3 Add the prepared salmon steaks and pineapple to the pan and bring to the boil. Reduce the heat to medium and cook, covered, for 10–12 minutes until the salmon turns opaque and is cooked through.

4 Remove the lid and carefully push the salmon and pineapple around the pan until well coated with the sauce. Remove the string from the steaks and serve immediately with the pineapple and sauce spooned over, with boiled rice, if you like.

CHA CA LA VONG

SERVES 4
PREPARATION TIME 25 minutes,
plus 30 minutes
marinating time
COOKING TIME 15–20 minutes

3cm/1¼in piece of fresh
turmeric, peeled and
roughly chopped, or 2 tsp
ground turmeric
1cm/½in piece of galangal,
peeled and chopped
1cm/½in piece of fresh
ginger, peeled and chopped
2 garlic cloves, chopped
2 tbsp fish sauce
2 tsp sugar
a generous pinch of ground
white pepper
550g/1lb 4oz skinned
monkfish, cod or pollack
fillets, cut into bite-size
pieces
185g/6½oz dried rice
vermicelli
3 tbsp sunflower oil
40g/1½oz dill, trimmed
10 spring onions/scallions,
cut into 6cm/2½in lengths
and sliced
15g/½oz chives, cut into
5cm/2in lengths (optional)

TO SERVE
50g/1¾oz/⅓ cup skinless
raw peanuts
1 small handful of Thai basil
leaves
1 small handful of coriander/
cilantro leaves
2 red chillies, deseeded and
sliced (optional)
1 recipe quantity Nuoc Cham
Dipping Sauce (*see page 236*)

1 Put the fresh turmeric, if using, galangal, ginger and garlic in a mortar or a food processor and pound with a pestle or blend into a smooth paste. Transfer to a large bowl, add the ground turmeric, if using, and combine with the fish sauce, sugar and ground pepper. Tip the fish into the bowl and toss until each piece of fish is well coated in the paste. Cover with cling film/plastic wrap and leave to marinate at room temperature for about 30 minutes.

2 Heat a frying pan over a medium-high heat, then add the peanuts and dry-roast until fragrant and starting to brown. Remove from the heat, roughly chop and leave to one side.

3 Bring a saucepan of water to the boil and cook the rice vermicelli for 2–3 minutes until softened. Drain, refresh under running cold water, pat dry with paper towels and divide into four individual serving bowls.

4 Heat the oil in a frying pan over a medium-high heat. Add the marinated fish and fry, stirring occasionally, for 6–7 minutes until crisp, golden brown and cooked through. Add the dill, spring onions and chives, if using. Toss and cook for a few more seconds until wilted. Remove from the heat and transfer to a serving dish.

5 Transfer the bowls of noodles, accompaniments and turmeric fish to the table for everyone to assemble their own dish.

CURRY FISH mousse

SERVES **6**
PREPARATION TIME **10 minutes**
COOKING TIME **20 minutes**

350ml/12fl oz/scant 1½ cups
   coconut milk
1 tbsp grated palm sugar or
   soft light brown sugar
1 tbsp fish sauce
1 recipe quantity Curry Fish
   Mousse Spice Paste (*see
   page 227*)
2 eggs, beaten
2 kaffir lime leaves, thinly
   sliced
450g/1lb boneless, skinless
   haddock loin, or other
   white fish fillets, cut into
   bite-size pieces
sea salt

TO SERVE
Tomato & Glass Noodle
   Salad (*see page 178*)

Traditionally, this Cambodian dish is served in banana leaves that are folded into a tray shape. Two leaves, cut into squares, are layered and then folded up at the edges to create corners, which are secured with cocktail sticks. A simpler way to serve Amok Trey is in small, heatproof bowls.

1 Put the coconut milk and sugar in a large bowl and stir until the sugar is dissolved. Add the fish sauce, spice paste, eggs, kaffir lime leaves and a pinch of salt and stir until combined. Tip in the fish and toss until the fish is well coated with the paste mixture.

2 Make up six banana leaf bowls (see introduction above), if you like, then fill with the coated fish – the sauce should nearly cover all the fish pieces. Alternatively, use six individual 150ml/5fl oz/scant ⅔ cup ramekins or heatproof bowls.

3 Place the leaf bowls or ramekins in a bamboo or electric steamer and steam for 20 minutes, or until the mixture is set and the fish is cooked through. It should be slightly firm to the touch. Leave to stand for 5 minutes at room temperature before serving with the Tomato & Glass Noodle Salad.

HOT & SPICY VEGETABLE STEW

SERVES 4
PREPARATION TIME 30 minutes, plus making the pork stock, if using
COOKING TIME about 1 hour

1 litre/35fl oz/4 cups vegetable stock or ½ recipe quantity Pork Stock (*see page 232*)
1 onion
2 star anise
¼ tsp black peppercorns
1 tbsp sunflower oil
2–2½ tsp chilli flakes, to taste
1 garlic clove, finely chopped
100g/3½oz baby corn, sliced in half lengthways
4 tomatoes, cut into wedges
100g/3½oz dried mushrooms, such as shiitake, porcini or Chinese mushrooms, soaked, drained and cut into thin strips (*see page 240*)
55g/2oz mangetout/snow peas
1 tbsp fish sauce
½ tsp sea salt
2 tbsp lime juice
1 tbsp grated palm sugar or soft light brown sugar

TO SERVE
350g/12oz cooked rice noodles (*see page 238*)
1 handful of coriander/ cilantro leaves

This Cambodian dish is one of the simplest and tastiest clear broth stews that I have ever eaten. It is a little like the Thai version Tom Yum. The combination of the spiciness from the chilli with the meatiness of the mushrooms and baby corn makes it filling and satisfying.

1 Pour the stock into a saucepan and bring to the boil over a high heat. Reduce the heat to low and simmer. Meanwhile, dry-fry the whole onion in a frying pan over a medium-high heat until the outer layer is slightly charred all round, then add the charred onion to the simmering stock. Put the star anise and peppercorns in a spice bag or secure in a piece of muslin/cheesecloth and add to the stock.

2 Heat the oil in a frying pan over a medium-high heat. Add the chilli flakes and garlic and stir-fry for 1–2 minutes until fragrant, then add to the stock. Continue to simmer the stock for 40 minutes. Discard the onion and the spice bag.

3 Just before serving, bring the stock to a gentle boil. Add the baby corn and tomatoes and cook for 2–3 minutes until they start to soften. Add the mushrooms and mangetout and cook for a further 2–3 minutes, or until all the vegetables are softened. Add the fish sauce, salt, lime juice and sugar and stir until the sugar is dissolved.

4 Bring the stew to a vigorous boil for a few seconds, then serve immediately with the rice noodles and with the coriander sprinkled over.

tomato & glass noodle salad

For a salad that is so easy to make, you will be surprised by just how satisfying and enjoyable it is to eat. The dressing is made up of punchy flavours, including unripened tomatoes, which are slightly more acidic than ripe ones and are often used in Cambodian cooking. If you can't get unripened tomatoes, cherry tomatoes are a good substitute.

SERVES **4**
PREPARATION TIME **30 minutes**
COOKING TIME **5–10 minutes**

150g/5½oz glass noodles, such as bean thread vermicelli
55g/2oz/⅓ cup raw cashew nuts
a generous pinch of chilli powder
2 tsp honey
300g/10½oz unripened tomatoes, roughly chopped, or cherry tomatoes, halved
½ red onion, finely sliced
85g/3oz/scant ½ cup bean sprouts
1 handful of coriander/ cilantro leaves
1 handful of Thai basil leaves or sweet basil leaves

DRESSING
1 garlic clove, finely chopped
2 red bird's eye chillies, deseeded and sliced
4 tbsp lime juice
½ tsp lime zest
4 tbsp fish sauce
2 tbsp clear honey

1 To make the dressing, put all the ingredients in a small bowl and gently whisk until combined. Leave to one side.

2 Bring a saucepan of water to the boil and cook the glass noodles for 2–3 minutes until softened. Drain, refresh under running cold water, pat dry with paper towels and tip into a large bowl.

3 Heat a frying pan over a medium-high heat, then add the cashew nuts and dry-roast until fragrant and starting to brown. Remove from the heat, add the chilli powder and honey to the pan and stir until the cashews are well coated. Leave to cool. When the nuts are cold enough to handle, roughly chop.

4 Add the tomatoes, onion, bean sprouts, coriander and Thai basil or sweet basil to the bowl with the prepared noodles. Pour over the dressing and toss all the ingredients together until well combined. Serve with the chopped spicy cashew nuts sprinkled over.

FRIED SPRING ROLLS

MAKES **12**
PREPARATION TIME **40 minutes**
COOKING TIME **25 minutes**

55g/2oz dried rice vermicelli
150g/5½oz minced/ground pork
150g/5½oz raw, peeled large king prawns/jumbo shrimp, deveined and cut into small pieces (*see page 241*)
1 garlic clove, finely chopped
2 spring onions/scallions, finely chopped
½ carrot, grated and excess liquid squeezed out
1 tbsp fish sauce
½ tsp granulated sugar
12 x 16cm/6¼in round rice paper sheets
500ml/17fl oz/2 cups sunflower oil, for deep-frying

TO SERVE
1 handful of fragrant herbs and salad leaves
1 recipe quantity Nuoc Cham Dipping Sauce (*see page 236*)

These crispy spring rolls never fail to impress all my friends when I make them! Take a salad leaf, put the spring roll and some herbs in the middle, then wrap it up and dip in the Nuoc Cham Dipping Sauce, which will give you a satisfying bite.

1 Bring a saucepan of water to the boil and cook the rice vermicelli for 2–3 minutes until softened. Drain, cool/refresh under running cold water, drain again and pat dry with paper towels. Roughly chop into small pieces and transfer to a mixing bowl.

2 Add the pork, king prawns, garlic, spring onions, carrot, fish sauce and sugar and mix until well combined. Divide the filling equally into 12 portions and set aside.

3 Lay a damp, clean dish towel on a chopping/cutting board and place a large bowl of warm water to the side. Take a sheet of rice paper and submerge in the warm water for about 10 seconds. Don't soak the rice paper for too long, otherwise it will tear.

4 Lay a soaked rice paper sheet flat on the damp dish towel. Take a portion of the filling and place it in the centre of the sheet. Mould into an oblong shape. Fold the bottom of the sheet over the filling, then fold in the two sides. Roll the spring roll as tightly as possible. Put the spring roll on a plate and cover with a damp, clean dish towel, then repeat until all the ingredients are used.

5 Heat the oil in a deep, heavy-based saucepan to 180°C/350°F, or until a small piece of bread turns brown in 15 seconds. Gently slide four rolls into the hot oil and deep-fry for about 5–7 minutes, or until the pork rolls are golden brown. Remove the rolls with a slotted spoon and drain on paper towels. Keep warm while you reheat the oil and deep-fry the remaining pork rolls in batches of four.

6 Serve hot with the fragrant herbs, salad leaves and Nuoc Cham Dipping Sauce on the side.

GRILLED BEEF SALAD

SERVES **4**
PREPARATION TIME **30 minutes,**
  plus 1 hour 25 minutes
  freezing and marinating
  time
COOKING TIME **about 10**
  minutes

4 garlic cloves, roughly
  chopped
3 shallots, roughly chopped
1cm/½in piece of fresh
  ginger, peeled and roughly
  chopped
1 red chilli, deseeded and
  roughly chopped
500g/1lb 2oz rib-eye steak
  or sirloin, wrapped and
  semi-frozen for 25 minutes
  (*see page 242*)
1 tbsp light soy sauce
½ tbsp grated palm sugar or
  soft light brown sugar
1 tbsp sunflower oil
1 star fruit
100g/3½oz/heaped ½ cup
  pomegranate seeds
1 small handful of coriander/
  cilantro leaves
1 tbsp mint leaves
2 tbsp Fried Shallots
  (*see page 235*), to serve

DRESSING
4 tbsp fish sauce
2 tbsp sugar
3 tbsp lime juice

I was treated to the best grilled beef salad I have ever eaten in Hanoi, Vietnam. The sweet, sour and salty dressing really complements the slightly charred beef slices, and the use of star fruit adds a delicious and unusual edge. If you can't get star fruit, substitute it with green apple. I've added pomegranate seeds and used coriander and mint, instead of the traditional Thai basil, to give this salad a refreshing twist.

1 Put the garlic, shallots, ginger and chilli in a mortar and pestle or a food processor and blend to a smooth paste. Transfer to a large bowl.

2 Remove the partially frozen beef from the freezer and unwrap the cling film/plastic wrap. Using a sharp knife, cut the beef against the grain into 3mm/⅛in slices. Put the beef in the bowl with the ground paste, then add the soy sauce and sugar and mix until well combined. Cover with cling film/plastic wrap and leave to marinate in the refrigerator for 1 hour.

3 Meanwhile, to prepare the dressing, mix all the ingredients with 4 tablespoons water and leave to one side.

4 Heat the oil in a ridged griddle pan or heavy-based frying pan over a high heat. When the oil is smoking hot, add the marinated beef and cook for a few seconds before turning the heat down to medium-high. Spread out the meat in the pan, laying it as flat as possible so it cooks evenly. Cook for 7–10 minutes, turning occasionally, until the beef is browned and tender.

5 Cut the star fruit into 5mm/¼in slices and put in a salad bowl. Add the pomegranate seeds, coriander, mint, stir-fried beef and dressing and toss well. Serve with the fried shallots sprinkled over.

Steamed rice cakes with prawns

MAKES 16
PREPARATION TIME 30 minutes,
plus cooling time
COOKING TIME about 30
minutes

150g/5½oz/heaped ¾ cup
rice flour
5 tsp cornflour/cornstarch
¼ tsp sea salt
3 tbsp sunflower oil, plus
extra for oiling
200g/7oz raw, peeled large
king prawns/jumbo shrimp,
deveined (*see page 241*)
2 garlic cloves, finely
chopped
2 shallots, finely diced
10g/¼oz pork rind, crushed
1 red chilli, deseeded and
finely sliced

SAUCE
1 tbsp fish sauce
2 tbsp clear honey

TO SERVE.
Dried rice vermicelli,
(see page 238)

**There are many amazing local specialities in Hue,
Vietnam, and I made sure I ate as many as I could during
my visit. These steamed rice cakes, Banh Beo, were my
favourite, and are great eaten as an afternoon snack.**

1 Put the rice flour, cornflour, salt and 1 tablespoon of the oil in a
bowl. Gradually pour in 350ml/12fl oz/scant 1½ cups water and mix
well. Leave to one side.

2 To make the sauce, put the fish sauce and honey in a small bowl
with 4 tablespoons water and gently whisk until combined. Leave to
one side.

3 Bring a saucepan of water to the boil. Add the prawns and cook for
3–4 minutes until they turn pink and are cooked through. Drain, dry
with paper towels and leave to cool. When cool, put the prawns in a
food processor and blend briefly – you still want some chunky bits.

4 Heat the remaining 2 tablespoons of oil in a frying pan over a
medium-high heat. Tip in the chopped prawns and stir-fry for
1 minute. Add the garlic and shallots and stir-fry for 4–5 minutes
until fragrant. Remove from the heat, cover and leave to one side.

5 Lightly oil 16 individual shallow dishes, such as dipping sauce dishes,
either all the same size or a range of sizes, if you like. Stir the rice
flour mixture until smooth, then divide into the dishes. Arrange as
many dishes as will fit in a bamboo or electric steamer and steam
for 8–10 minutes until set. Leave to cool, and repeat until all the
rice cakes are cooked.

6 Serve the rice cakes either in the dishes or gently scoop them out,
using a spoon, onto a serving plate. Put about 1 tablespoon of the
cooked prawn mixture on top of each rice cake and then sprinkle
over the crushed pork rind and chilli. Just before serving, drizzle
1–2 teaspoons of the sauce over each rice cake.

GRILLED PRAWN LEMONGRASS SKEWERS

In Vietnam these grilled prawn skewers are usually served on their own. For a more complete and moreish dish, I wrap the prawn meat in lettuce leaves with herbs and bean sprouts. Another way to make this dish is to wrap the prawn meat in dry rice paper. Because the rice paper isn't soaked, you get to enjoy the different textures of the ingredients – the crispiness of the rice paper, which is slightly softened by the Nuoc Cham Dipping Sauce, and the tender, moist prawns.

MAKES 16
PREPARATION TIME 30 minutes, plus 1 hour marinating time
COOKING TIME 30 minutes

500g/1lb 2oz raw, peeled large king prawns/jumbo shrimp, deveined and roughly chopped (see page 241)
2 garlic cloves, finely chopped
1 tbsp fish sauce
1 tsp grated palm sugar or soft light brown sugar
1 spring onion/scallion, chopped
1 tbsp sunflower oil, plus extra for oiling
16 lemongrass stalks, outer leaves and stalk ends removed, trimmed to 4.5cm/1¾in lengths
sea salt

TO SERVE
80g/2¾oz dried rice vermicelli
1 small round lettuce
6 sprigs Thai basil
1 small handful of pea shoots
55g/2oz/heaped ¼ cup bean sprouts
1 recipe quantity Nuoc Cham Dipping Sauce (see page 236)
Dried rice vermicelli, (see page 238)

1 Put the prawns, garlic, fish sauce, sugar and spring onion in a food processor and blend to a rough paste without any solid pieces of prawns. Transfer to a bowl and stir in the oil. Cover with cling film/plastic wrap and leave to marinate in the refrigerator for 1 hour.

2 Bring a saucepan of water to the boil and cook the vermicelli for 2–3 minutes until softened. Drain, refresh under running cold water, pat dry with paper towels and transfer to a serving plate.

3 Prepare a bowl of slightly salted water. Moisten one hand with the salted water to avoid the prawn paste sticking and then place 2 heaped tablespoons of the prawn paste in your palm. Use the back of the spoon to flatten the paste into a 5cm/2in circle, then slightly close your hand and place a lemongrass stalk along the centre. Mould the paste around the lemongrass. Set aside and repeat until all the ingredients are used.

4 Line a bamboo or electric steamer with a piece of greaseproof paper and arrange the prawn skewers on the paper. Steam the skewers for about 5 minutes, or until the prawn paste is almost cooked through. Remove from the heat and leave to stand at room temperature for 5 minutes.

5 Pour some oil into a ridged griddle pan or heavy-based frying pan over a medium-high heat, then use a paper towel to grease the pan evenly and soak up any excess oil. Grill the prawn skewers in batches of 5–6 sticks, turning frequently, for 6–7 minutes until browned all round and cooked through. Remove from the pan and keep warm until all the skewers are cooked. Oil the pan again, as required.

6 Transfer the skewers, accompaniments and Nuoc Cham Dipping Sauce to the table for everyone to make up into parcels and then dip in the sauce. To assemble the parcels, cut the prawn meat off the lemongrass and into smaller pieces and then fold up in a lettuce leaf with the herbs, bean sprouts and rice vermicelli.

VIETNAMESE PRAWN RICE PAPER ROLLS

MAKES 12
PREPARATION TIME 45 minutes
COOKING TIME 3 minutes

120g/4¼oz dried rice
  vermicelli
12 x 16cm/6¼in round rice
  paper sheets
36 Thai basil leaves or mint
  leaves
24 cooked, peeled large king
  prawns/jumbo shrimp
20g/¾oz/scant ¼ cup bean
  sprouts
24 garlic chives, cut into
  16cm/6¼in lengths

TO SERVE
1 recipe quantity Nuoc
  Cham Dipping Sauce (*see
  page 236*)

These spring rolls, neatly wrapped in translucent rice paper, look stunning with a hint of orange and green colours from the ingredients inside showing through. Each bite of these healthy finger foods, reveals a mouth-watering combination of the fresh, clean flavours of the rice paper rolls against the gentle tang of the Nuoc Cham Dipping Sauce.

1 Bring a saucepan of water to the boil and cook the rice vermicelli for 2–3 minutes until softened. Drain, refresh under running cold water and pat dry with paper towels. Transfer to a bowl and roughly cut into 6cm/2½in pieces.

2 Lay a damp, clean dish towel on a chopping/cutting board and place a large bowl of warm water to the side. Take a sheet of rice paper and submerge in the warm water for about 10 seconds. Don't soak the rice paper for too long, as it will tear.

3 Lay a soaked rice paper sheet flat on the dish towel. Arrange 3 basil leaves along the centre of the sheet, then place 2 prawns roughly on top of the basil leaves. Next put a few bean sprouts on the prawns and then a large pinch of cooked rice vermicelli. Mould the ingredients into an oblong shape. Fold the bottom of the sheet over the filling, then fold in the two sides. Add 2 garlic chives to the centre, crossways, so one end of each of the chives sticks over the edge. Roll the spring roll and chives up as tightly as possible. Put the spring roll on a serving plate and cover with a damp dish towel, then repeat until all the ingredients are used. Serve at room temperature with Nuoc Cham Dipping Sauce on the side.

VIETNAMESE SAGO PUDDING

SERVES 4
PREPARATION TIME **20 minutes,
plus dried bean soaking
and cooling time**
COOKING TIME **45 minutes**

250g/9oz/heaped 1 cup
caster/granulated sugar
85g/3oz/1⅓ cups medium
sago pearls
1 tsp green tea powder
100g/3½oz/scant ½ cup
peeled split mung beans,
soaked for at least 4 hours
or overnight
55g/2oz/¼ cup kidney
beans, soaked for 2 hours,
or 80g/2¾oz/heaped ⅓ cup
drained canned kidney
beans
150ml/5fl oz/scant ⅔ cup
coconut milk
¼ tsp fine sea salt
crushed ice, to serve

1 Put 200g/7oz/heaped ¾ cup of the sugar and 80ml/2½fl oz/
⅓ cup water in a saucepan over a medium-high heat. Bring to the
boil, stirring constantly to dissolve the sugar, then reduce the heat
to medium-low and gently boil for 6–7 minutes until the mixture
starts to thicken but not colour. Remove from the heat and leave
to one side.

2 Bring a large saucepan of water to the boil. Add the sago pearls,
reduce the heat to medium-low and cook for 30 minutes,
uncovered, or until they become translucent, stirring occasionally
to stop the pearls from sticking. Add more boiling water if the sago
gets too sticky. Drain in a colander and rinse under running cold
water, lightly rubbing the sago to wash away the starch. Transfer to
a bowl, sprinkle over the green tea powder and mix until well
combined. Leave to cool.

3 Meanwhile, cook the soaked and drained split mung beans and
kidney beans, if using. Put the split mung beans in a saucepan, add
150ml/5fl oz/scant ⅔ cup water and bring to the boil over a high
heat. Cover the pan, reduce the heat to medium and cook, stirring
occasionally, for 30 minutes or until the mung beans are soft and
almost falling apart. Add more water to the pan if the beans
become too dry. Remove from the heat, add the remaining sugar
and stir until well combined. Using a fork or potato masher, mash
the beans to a fine paste and leave to cool.

4 At the same time, bring a further saucepan of water to the boil over
a high heat and add the soaked and drained kidney beans. Cover
the pan, reduce the heat to medium and cook for 15–20 minutes
until tender. Remove from the heat, drain and leave to cool. If using
canned kidney beans, drain and rinse well.

5 While the beans are cooking, put the coconut milk and salt in a
saucepan and gently heat over a medium-low heat, stirring
occasionally. When bubbles start to form on the surface, remove
from the heat and leave to cool.

6 Divide the sugar syrup into 4 glasses. Add the mung beans, then
the coloured sago followed by the kidney beans. Top each glass with
the coconut milk, then add a large handful of crushed ice to each
glass just before serving. Give everything a good stir before eating.

INDIA & SRI LANKA

India is a vast country where the food varies greatly regionally. In the northern regions, the food is generally creamy, rich and flavoursome but mildly spicy, as in Lamb Rogan Josh (*see page 202*), whereas in the southern parts dishes are often significantly more spicy and are mostly coconut based, as in Fish Curry with Okra (*see page 208*) and Kerala Beef (*see page 200*). But no matter which part of India you are in, dried spices of many varieties come into play. Before the cooking starts, there is the grinding and toasting of the spices, and this step makes a real difference to the taste of the final dish.

Similarly in Sri Lanka, the use of dried spices, such as cardamom, cinnamon, cloves, cumin, ground fennel, pepper and turmeric is key, but in comparison to India, there are fewer fresh spices used, mainly just chilli and curry leaves. However, despite this, there is a beautiful, subtle boldness and balance to Sri Lankan cuisine, and Sour Fish Curry (*see page 207*) is an amazing example. Pandan leaves, which grow luxuriantly in most backyards in Sri Lanka, are one of the most important items when cooking traditional Sri Lankan curries, such as Devilled Pork (*see page 198*), and provide a unique, flowery fragrance and flavour. A delicious modern twist to these dishes is to use lemongrass instead.

CHICKEN BIRYANI RICE

SERVES 4
PREPARATION TIME 30 minutes,
  plus about 1 hour
  marinating, soaking and
  resting time
COOKING TIME about 1 hour

600g/1lb 5oz boneless,
  skinless chicken thighs,
  cut into bite-size pieces
½ tsp ground turmeric
¼ tsp chilli powder
2 garlic cloves, grated
2 tbsp Greek yogurt
1 tsp sea salt
350g/12oz/1¾ cups basmati
  rice
¼ tsp cumin seeds
2 x 5cm/2in cinnamon sticks
6 green cardamom pods
2 tbsp sunflower oil
2 black cardamom pods
4 cloves
3–4 dried bay leaves
1 star anise
6–7 black peppercorns
2 onions, sliced
2 green chillies, deseeded
  and chopped
1 tomato, chopped
½ tsp tomato purée/paste
a pinch of saffron threads
1 tbsp butter, softened
1 handful of coriander/
  cilantro leaves, roughly
  chopped, to serve
1–2 tbsp desiccated/dried
  shredded coconut, to serve
2 tbsp Fried Shallots (see
  page 235), to serve

Biryani, a meal in itself, originates from Persia and is a highly celebrated dish in India. Don't be put off by the long list of spices. The time and effort you put into preparing this dish will definitely be repaid in the eating.

1 Put the chicken pieces in a large bowl, then add the turmeric, chilli powder, garlic, yogurt and ½ teaspoon of the salt and toss until each piece of chicken is well coated with the marinade. Cover with cling film/plastic wrap and leave to marinate in the refrigerator for 45 minutes–1 hour. Remove from the refrigerator and leave to stand at room temperature for 15 minutes before cooking.

2 Meanwhile, put the rice in a large saucepan and pour in enough water to half fill the pan. Swirl the rice using your hand, lightly rubbing the grains, until the water becomes cloudy. Tilt the pot carefully to pour off the water. Repeat this process 3–4 times. The water will not be completely clear, but will be less cloudy than the first wash. Cover the rice with water and leave to stand for 30 minutes. Drain and leave to sit in the sieve for 5 minutes.

3 Half fill a saucepan with water and bring to the boil over a medium-high heat. Add the washed rice, cumin seeds, 1 cinnamon stick, 3 green cardamom pods and the remaining ½ teaspoon of salt and boil gently for 3–4 minutes. Drain the rice into a sieve and rinse under running cold water to stop the cooking process. Discard the cinnamon stick and cardamom pods and leave to one side.

4 Heat the oil in a large, heavy-based frying pan over a medium heat. Add the remaining cinnamon stick and 3 green cardamom pods, the black cardamom pods, cloves, bay leaves, star anise and peppercorns and sizzle for a few seconds until fragrant. Add the onions and stir-fry for 3–4 minutes until soft and translucent. Tip in the chillies, tomato and tomato purée and stir-fry for 1–2 minutes.

5 Tip in the chicken and push around the pan until well coated with the spices. Cook for 10–15 minutes until the chicken is sealed and golden brown, stirring occasionally. Meanwhile, put the saffron threads in a bowl with 2 tablespoons hot water and leave to one side.

6 When the chicken is cooked, remove the pan from the heat and transfer the chicken and all the pan ingredients to a plate. Using the same pan, spread half of the partially cooked rice evenly over the base. Drizzle 1 tablespoon of the saffron liquid over the rice, then arrange half of the chicken pieces on top of the rice. Spread the remaining rice evenly over the chicken, drizzle over the remaining saffron liquid and add the remaining chicken. Sprinkle about 30ml/1fl oz/2 tablespoons water into the pan and scatter over the butter.

7 Place the pan over a low heat, cover and cook for 30 minutes, or until the rice is cooked and the chicken tender. About 15 minutes into the cooking time, give the rice and chicken a quick and thorough stir. Serve hot with the coriander, desiccated coconut and fried shallots sprinkled over.

COORG-STYLE CHICKEN CURRY

Coorg is situated in South West India, and the cuisine in this area of India is very much influenced by its geography, culture and people. In general, curries are slightly spicier, and coconut milk is used more often than in curries from other parts of India.

SERVES 4
PREPARATION TIME 25 minutes, plus 30 minutes marinating time
COOKING TIME about 45 minutes

500g/1lb 2oz boneless, skinless chicken breasts or chicken thighs, trimmed and cut into bite-size pieces
½ tsp ground turmeric
½ tsp chilli powder
2 tbsp sunflower oil
½ tsp black mustard seeds
1 red onion, chopped
2 garlic cloves, finely chopped
3cm/1¼in piece of fresh ginger, peeled and grated
1 recipe quantity Coorg-style Curry Spice Paste (*see page 227*)
3 tomatoes, skinned, halved, deseeded and roughly chopped (*see page 242*)
2 tbsp lime juice
100ml/3½fl oz/generous ⅓ cup coconut milk
sea salt

TO SERVE
1 small handful of coriander/ cilantro leaves
1 recipe quantity Boiled Long-Grain Rice (*see page 237*)
Garlic Naan (*see page 196*)

1 Put the chicken in a large bowl, then add the turmeric, chilli powder and a pinch of salt and toss until each of the chicken pieces is well coated with the spices. Cover with cling film/plastic wrap and leave to marinate for 30 minutes at room temperature.

2 Heat the oil in a frying pan over a medium-high heat. Add the mustard seeds and sizzle for about 30 seconds until fragrant, then add the onion and stir-fry for 2–3 minutes until soft and translucent. Add the garlic and ginger and stir-fry for 1 minute. Add the spice paste and cook gently, stirring occasionally, for 2–3 minutes until fragrant.

3 Tip in the marinated chicken pieces and stir-fry for 5–7 minutes until they turn opaque. Stir in the tomatoes, then add the lime juice and 100ml/3½fl oz/generous ⅓ cup water and bring to the boil. Add the coconut milk, stir to combine and then bring to a gentle boil. Reduce the heat to low and simmer, covered, for 15–20 minutes until the sauce starts to thicken and the chicken is cooked through. Serve hot with the coriander sprinkled over and either boiled rice or Garlic Naan on the side.

tandoori chicken with garlic naan

This is one of the most popular dishes in Indian cuisine. The chicken is tenderized with yogurt, aromatic spices and roots, and a little red food colouring is added to give the trademark bright red appearance. Here, however, I am using ground saffron to give it a slightly different edge. This well-flavoured chicken is especially good with naan bread, and I've included the recipe for Garlic Naan. If you prefer, you could replace the garlic with fresh herbs for a herb-flavoured naan.

SERVES 6
PREPARATION TIME 30 minutes, plus minimum 5 hours 30 minutes marinating and resting time
COOKING TIME 1 hour 15 minutes

TANDOORI CHICKEN
6 chicken legs, skin removed
5 tbsp yogurt
4 garlic cloves, grated
2cm/¾in piece of fresh ginger, peeled and grated
2 tsp chilli powder
1 tsp paprika
2 tsp ground cumin
2 tsp ground turmeric
1 tbsp ground coriander
½ tsp ground black pepper
¼ tsp ground saffron
½ tsp sea salt
juice of ½ lime
1 tbsp sunflower oil
30g/1oz butter, softened
1 handful of coriander/cilantro leaves, chopped, to serve
1 onion, sliced, to serve
1 lime, cut into wedges, to serve

GARLIC NAAN
1 tsp granulated sugar
1 tsp dried active yeast
350g/12oz/heaped 2¾ cups plain/all-purpose flour, plus extra for dusting
1 tsp baking powder
¼ tsp fine sea salt
6 garlic cloves, finely chopped
55g/2oz butter, melted, plus extra for greasing

1 Transfer the chicken legs to a chopping/cutting board and then, using a sharp knife, make 3 long, deep diagonal slits into the thigh area of the legs and 3 smaller ones into the drumsticks.

2 Put all the remaining tandoori chicken ingredients, except the butter, in a large bowl and mix well to make a paste. Add the chicken legs and rub the paste into the chicken until it is well coated. Cover with cling film/plastic wrap and leave to marinate in the refrigerator for 5–6 hours or, for an even better flavour, overnight.

3 To make the naan dough, stir the sugar and yeast into 200ml/7fl oz/scant 1 cup water until the sugar is dissolved. Leave to stand for 10 minutes or until foaming. Sift the flour into a large mixing bowl and then mix in the baking powder, salt and garlic. Make a well in the centre and pour in the melted butter. Slowly pour in the water mixture and combine with the other ingredients to form a soft dough. Add extra flour if the dough is too sticky. Turn the dough out onto a lightly floured surface and knead for 10 minutes until it is smooth and elastic. Place the dough back in the bowl, cover with a damp dish towel and leave to stand in a warm place for 1–1½ hours, or until the dough has doubled in size.

4 Turn the risen dough onto a lightly floured surface and divide into 2 portions. Knead each portion for 2 minutes, roll into a cylinder and divide into 5 equal pieces. Keeping the dough that you are not using covered with a damp dish towel, shape a dough piece into a ball and then flatten using your hand. Using a rolling pin, roll the dough into a 13cm/5in disc about 5mm/¼in thick. Put the disc on a floured tray, cover with a damp dish towel and repeat for the remaining dough balls.

5 Heat a griddle pan or heavy-based frying pan over a high heat and grease with a little melted butter. Add a portion of dough and cook for 3–4 minutes on each side until it blisters and brown spots form. When cooked, melt a small knob/pat of butter on both sides of the naan, then transfer it to a heatproof tray and keep warm. Repeat until all the naan are cooked.

6 Meanwhile, remove the marinated chicken from the refrigerator, pour off any excess liquid and leave to stand at room temperature for 25–30 minutes before cooking. Preheat the oven to 200°C/400°F/Gas 6. Place a roasting rack on a baking sheet and arrange the chicken legs on the rack. Smear some of the butter over each chicken leg, then put in the oven for 30–35 minutes until cooked through. When the tip of a sharp knife is inserted into the thickest part of the meat, the juices should run clear. Serve hot with the coriander and onion sprinkled over the top and the naan and lime wedges on the side.

DeVILLeD PORK

In this Sri Lankan dish, the meat is slowly cooked in a well-flavoured sauce – the richness and depth of aromas develop and the tender meat melts in your mouth.

SERVES 4–6
PREPARATION TIME **20 minutes**
COOKING TIME **1 hour 25 minutes**

2 tbsp sunflower oil
2 sprigs curry leaves
2 black cardamom pods
2 cloves
5cm/2in cinnamon stick
1 onion, chopped
2 green chillies, deseeded and halved
4 garlic cloves, finely chopped
2cm/¾in piece of fresh ginger, peeled and grated
1 tsp chilli powder
1 tsp ground turmeric
½ tsp ground cumin
1 tsp ground coriander
800g/1lb 12oz deboned pork shoulder, trimmed and cut into bite-size pieces
2 tomatoes, skinned and roughly chopped (see page 242)
3 lemongrass stalks, outer leaves and stalk ends removed and crushed, or 3 pandan leaves, tied into a knot
½ tsp sea salt
1 tbsp lime juice

TO SERVE
1 recipe quantity Boiled Long-Grain Rice (see page 237)

1 Heat the oil in a large, heavy-based saucepan over a medium-high heat. Add the curry leaves, cardamom pods, cloves and cinnamon stick and sizzle for a few seconds, then add the onion and stir-fry for 2–3 minutes until soft and translucent. Add the chillies, garlic and ginger and stir-fry for 1–2 minutes until fragrant. Add the chilli powder, turmeric, cumin and coriander and stir-fry for 1 minute. Tip in the pork, tomatoes, lemongrass stalks or pandan leaves and salt and toss until the pork is well coated with the spices.

2 Pour in the lime juice and 550ml/19fl oz/scant 2¼ cups water, increase the heat to high and bring to the boil. Cover the pan, reduce the heat to low and simmer for 1 hour 15 minutes, or until the pork is tender and the sauce has thickened, stirring occasionally. Serve hot with boiled rice.

SERVES 4
PREPARATION TIME 35 minutes,
  plus 30 minutes
  marinating time
COOKING TIME about 45
  minutes

500g/1lb 2oz beef fillet, cut
  into bite-size pieces
3 garlic cloves, finely grated
5mm/¼in piece of fresh
  ginger, peeled and grated
1 tsp ground turmeric
¼ tsp freshly ground black
  pepper
2 tsp ground coriander
2 tsp ground cumin
2 tsp chilli powder
1 tbsp sunflower oil
1 onion, chopped
2 green bird's eye chillies,
  whole
2 sprigs curry leaves
1 tomato, skinned and
  roughly chopped (*see
  page 242*)
15g/½oz coconut flesh,
  thinly sliced (*see page
  240*), or desiccated/dried
  shredded coconut, plus
  extra to serve
sea salt

TO SERVE
1 recipe quantity Boiled
  Long-Grain Rice
  (*see page 237*)

Kerala Beef

Kerala is in South West India, and this is a great curry standby from the region, as it is can be whipped up quickly and then left on the hob to cook. The fresh coconut provides depth of flavour and also helps to thicken the sauce.

1 Put the beef in a bowl, add the garlic, ginger, turmeric, pepper, coriander, cumin and chilli powder and toss until the beef is well coated with the spices. Season with salt, then cover with cling film/plastic wrap and leave to marinate for 30 minutes at room temperature.

2 Heat the oil in a heavy-based saucepan over a medium-high heat. Add the onion, chillies and curry leaves and stir-fry for 2–3 minutes until the onions are soft and translucent. Tip in the marinated beef, toss until the beef is well coated with all the other ingredients and cook for 5 minutes, stirring occasionally.

3 Add the tomato and coconut. Pour in 150ml/5fl oz/scant ⅔ cup water and stir well. Bring to the boil, then reduce the heat to low and simmer for 30–35 minutes until the beef is tender and the sauce starts to thicken, stirring occasionally. Serve warm with extra coconut sprinkled over and boiled rice.

LAMB ROGAN JOSH

Of Kashmir origin, Rogan Josh has become a favourite dish in both India and Pakistan. Very aromatic, there is no secret to this dish – the meat gets its flavour from the many spices used. The yogurt helps to tenderize the meat and is the base for the creamy sauce that coats it.

SERVES 4
PREPARATION TIME 15 minutes, plus minimum 2 hours marinating time
COOKING TIME about 1 hour

600g/1lb 5oz deboned lamb shoulder, trimmed and cut into bite-size pieces
1 tsp chilli powder
1 tsp ground turmeric
100g/3½oz/scant ½ cup Greek yogurt
5 green cardamom pods
½ tsp black peppercorns
5–6 cloves
1 star anise
3cm/1¼in cinnamon stick
3–4 dried bay leaves
1 tbsp ground coriander
½ tbsp ground cumin
1 tbsp sunflower oil
2 onions, chopped
5 garlic cloves, finely chopped
3cm/1¼in piece of fresh ginger, peeled and grated
1 tbsp tomato purée/paste

TO SERVE
1 small handful of coriander/ cilantro leaves
1 lime, cut into wedges
1 recipe quantity Boiled Long-Grain Rice (*see page 237*)

1 Put the lamb in a large bowl, then add the chilli powder, turmeric and yogurt and toss until all the pieces of lamb are well coated with the marinade. Cover with cling film/plastic wrap and leave to marinate in the refrigerator for 2–3 hours or, for an even better flavour, overnight.

2 Put the cardamom pods, peppercorns, cloves, star anise, cinnamon stick and bay leaves in a food processor or coffee grinder and grind until powdery. Transfer the spices to a bowl and add the ground coriander and cumin. Heat a frying pan over a medium heat, then add the spice powder and dry-fry, stirring frequently, for 2–3 minutes until aromatic. Leave to one side to cool.

3 Heat the oil in a heavy-based saucepan over a medium heat. Add the spice powder and sizzle for a few seconds, then add the onions and stir-fry for 2–3 minutes until soft and translucent. Add the garlic and ginger and stir-fry for 1–2 minutes until fragrant. Tip in the marinated lamb, push around the pan until well coated with the spices, then cook for 15–20 minutes, or until the meat is sealed and browned, stirring occasionally.

4 Add 150ml/5fl oz/scant ⅔ cup water, bring to the boil for a few seconds, skim any fat or scum off the surface and add the tomato purée. Reduce the heat to low and simmer for 20–25 minutes until the meat is tender and almost falling apart. About 15 minutes into cooking, or when the pork becomes slightly dry, add another 100ml/3½fl oz/generous ⅓ cup water. Serve warm with the coriander sprinkled over, lime wedges on the side and boiled rice.

LAMB KORMA

SERVES **4**
PREPARATION TIME **15 minutes,**
  plus 30 minutes
  marinating time
COOKING TIME **about 2 hours**
  15 minutes

700g/1lb 9oz deboned lamb
  shoulder, trimmed and cut
  into bite-size pieces
1 tsp ground turmeric
2 tbsp sunflower oil
5cm/2in cinnamon stick
½ tsp black mustard seeds
2 cloves
3 green cardamom pods
2 star anise
3–4 black peppercorns
1 onion, roughly chopped
2cm/¾in piece of fresh
  ginger, peeled and grated
4 garlic cloves, finely
  chopped
2 red chillies, deseeded and
  halved lengthways
1 tsp ground coriander
½ tsp ground cumin
2 tomatoes, skinned and
  roughly chopped (*see page
  242*)
1 tbsp tomato purée/paste
150ml/5fl oz/scant ⅔ cup
  coconut milk
½ tsp sea salt
200g/7oz butternut squash,
  deseeded, peeled and cut
  into wedges

TO SERVE
1 handful of coriander/
  cilantro leaves, chopped
1 recipe quantity Boiled
  Long-Grain Rice (*see
  page 237*)

1 Put the lamb in a large bowl, then add the turmeric and toss until all the pieces of lamb are well coated with the spices. Cover with cling film/plastic wrap and leave to marinate for 30 minutes at room temperature.

2 Heat the oil in a large saucepan over a medium heat. Add the cinnamon stick, mustard seeds, cloves, cardamom pods, star anise and peppercorns and sizzle for a few seconds until fragrant, then add the onion and stir-fry for 2–3 minutes until soft and translucent. Add the ginger, garlic and chillies and stir-fry for 2–3 minutes until fragrant, then add the coriander, cumin, tomatoes and tomato purée and mix well. Tip in the marinated lamb, toss until the lamb is well coated with all the other ingredients, then cook for 15–20 minutes until the meat is sealed and browned, stirring occasionally.

3 Add the coconut milk, salt and 500ml/17fl oz/2 cups water to the pan, mix well and bring to the boil. Reduce the heat to low and simmer, uncovered, for 30 minutes, then add the butternut squash and toss until well coated with the sauce. Simmer for a further 1 hour 15 minutes, or until the meat is tender. Serve hot with the coriander sprinkled over and boiled rice.

SOUR FISH CURRY

SERVES **4**
PREPARATION TIME **10** minutes
COOKING TIME **15–25** minutes

2 tbsp sunflower oil
2 cloves
2 green cardamom pods
1 red onion, roughly chopped
2 sprigs curry leaves
1 recipe quantity Sour Fish Curry Spice Paste (*see page 230*)
1 tomato, skinned and roughly chopped (*see page 242*)
1 tbsp lime juice or ½ recipe quantity Tamarind Water (*see page 242*)
1 tbsp clear honey
500g/1lb 2oz boneless, skinless tuna or salmon steaks, cut into bite-size pieces
sea salt

TO SERVE
1 recipe quantity Boiled Long-Grain Rice (*see page 237*)

This is a Sri Lankan speciality. An island nation, Sri Lanka is surrounded by the Indian Ocean where fish like tuna is abundant. Spices and fish go very well together, as the bolder touches of fragrant spices really complement the more subtle flavours of fish.

1 Heat the oil in a heavy-based saucepan over a medium-high heat. Add the cloves and cardamom pods and sizzle for a few seconds, then add the onion and curry leaves and stir-fry for 2–3 minutes until the onion is soft and translucent. Add the spice paste and cook for 5–7 minutes until fragrant, stirring occasionally, then add the tomato and cook for a further 5 minutes.

2 Add the lime juice and 100ml/3½fl oz/generous ⅓ cup water and bring to the boil. Stir in the honey and tuna or salmon and season with salt, then reduce the heat to low and simmer, stirring occasionally, for 5–10 minutes until the fish is cooked through and the liquid has started to evaporate. Serve hot with boiled rice.

SERVES **4**
PREPARATION TIME **20 minutes**
COOKING TIME **25 minutes**

2 tbsp sunflower oil
¼ tsp black mustard seeds
3 sprigs curry leaves
1 red onion, sliced into rings
2 garlic cloves, finely
  chopped
1cm/½in piece of fresh
  ginger, peeled and finely
  grated
1 tsp ground coriander
½ tsp ground cumin
2 tsp chilli powder
½ tsp ground turmeric
½ tsp sea salt
1 tsp clear honey
1 tbsp lime juice
2 tomatoes, skinned and
  quartered (*see page 242*)
250ml/9fl oz/1 cup coconut
  milk
85g/3oz okra
2 mackerels, scaled and
  gutted by your fishmonger
  and cut into 3cm/1¼in
  steaks

TO SERVE
1 recipe quantity Boiled
  Long-Grain Rice
  (*see page 237*)

FISH CURRY WITH OKRA

Okra, also known as lady's fingers, are a great addition to curry dishes, because they go extremely well with spices. Raw, they have a crunchy texture, but when cooked the pods turn soft and gummy inside, and really soak up the flavours of the sauce.

1 Heat the oil in a large saucepan over a medium-high heat. Add the mustard seeds and sizzle for a few seconds, then add the curry leaves and cook for 1 minute until fragrant. Add the onion, garlic and ginger and stir-fry for 2–3 minutes until fragrant and the onion is soft and translucent. Stir in the coriander, cumin, chilli powder, turmeric, salt, honey and lime juice, then add the tomatoes and mix well.

2 Pour the coconut milk and 60ml/2fl oz/¼ cup water into the pan and bring to the boil, then add the okra, reduce the heat to low, cover and simmer for 10–15 minutes until tender, stirring occasionally. Add the mackerel steaks and cook for 5 minutes, or until the flesh turns opaque, stirring occasionally. Serve hot with boiled rice.

PRAWN CURRY

SERVES 4
PREPARATION TIME 30 minutes
COOKING TIME 15–20 minutes

1 tbsp sunflower oil
¼ tsp black mustard seeds
2 sprigs curry leaves
1 onion, chopped
2 garlic cloves, finely
  chopped
1cm/½in piece of fresh
  ginger, peeled and finely
  chopped
1 tsp chilli powder
½ tsp ground turmeric
1 tsp ground coriander
¼ tsp ground cinnamon
½ tsp ground cumin
½ tsp sea salt
1 tsp granulated sugar
1 tbsp lime juice
200ml/7fl oz/scant 1 cup
  coconut milk
500g/1lb 2oz raw, unpeeled
  large king prawns/jumbo
  shrimp

TO SERVE
1 tbsp coriander/cilantro
  leaves
1 recipe quantity Boiled
  Long-Grain Rice
  (see page 237)

If you love seafood you will love this Indian dish, which has mild but deep, aromatic flavours. The prawns are cooked unpeeled, adding an extra sweetness to the curry sauce, while the coconut milk adds a silkiness. If you prefer a spicy curry, replace the chilli powder in the spice paste with ground, dried chillies – a guaranteed spice kick!

1 Heat the oil in a heavy-based saucepan over a medium-high heat. Add the black mustard seeds and sizzle for a few seconds, then add the curry leaves and cook for 1 minute until fragrant. Add the onion, garlic and ginger and stir-fry for 3–5 minutes until fragrant and the onion is soft and translucent.

2 Add the chilli powder, turmeric, ground coriander, cinnamon, cumin, salt, sugar and lime juice to the pan and stir until all the ingredients are well combined. Pour in the coconut milk and bring to the boil, then reduce the heat to low. Add the prawns, stirring until well coated with the sauce, then cover and simmer for 5–10 minutes until the prawns turn pink and are cooked through, stirring occasionally. Serve immediately with the coriander sprinkled over and boiled rice.

PANEER & SPINACH CURRY

This is a hearty northern Indian dish that is flavoured with spices, and has a rich and creamy tomato and spinach based gravy. The mild Indian cheese is pan-fried to add some crispiness to its outer layer, then cooked and coated with the aromatic sauce. It is delicious and suitable for vegetarians.

SERVES **4**
PREPARATION TIME **15 minutes**
COOKING TIME **20–25 minutes**

150g/5½oz baby leaf spinach
2 tbsp sunflower oil
250g/9oz paneer cheese, cubed
2 onions, chopped
2 green chillies, deseeded and halved lengthways
2 garlic cloves, finely chopped
1cm/½in piece of fresh ginger, peeled and grated
1 tsp ground coriander
1 tsp ground cumin
1 tsp ground turmeric
½ tsp chilli powder
3 tomatoes, skinned and roughly chopped (*see page 242*)
sea salt

TO SERVE
1 recipe quantity Boiled Long-Grain Rice (*see page 237*)

1 Bring a saucepan of water to the boil, add the spinach and blanch for 1 minute. Drain, squeezing out as much water as possible, then transfer the spinach to a food processor and blend to a smooth paste. Leave to one side.

2 Heat 1 tablespoon of the oil in a frying pan over a medium-high heat. Add the paneer and fry, stirring frequently, for 6–8 minutes until brown all round. Leave to one side.

3 Heat the remaining tablespoon of oil in a saucepan over a medium-high heat. Add the onions and chillies and stir-fry for 2–3 minutes until the onions are soft and translucent. Add the garlic and ginger and stir-fry for 1–2 minutes until fragrant, then stir in the coriander, cumin, turmeric and chilli powder. Add the tomatoes, spinach paste and 55ml/1¾fl oz/scant ¼ cup water and bring to the boil. Reduce the heat to low and simmer for 10 minutes, or until the sauce is thickened, stirring occasionally. Add the paneer, stir to combine with the sauce and season with salt. Serve hot with boiled rice.

Cashew & Coconut Curry

SERVES 4–6
PREPARATION TIME 15 minutes
COOKING TIME about 45 minutes

1 tsp ground coriander
½ tsp ground cumin
1 tsp ground turmeric
2 tbsp sunflower oil
1 onion, chopped
2 lemongrass stalks, outer leaves and stalk ends removed and crushed, or 2 pandan leaves, tied into a knot
5cm/2in cinnamon stick
2cm/¾in piece of fresh ginger, peeled and grated
3 garlic cloves, finely minced
1 tsp chilli powder
½ tsp freshly ground black pepper
300g/10½oz/scant 2 cups cashew nuts
350ml/12fl oz/scant 1½ cups coconut milk
1 tsp granulated sugar
1 tsp sea salt
1 handful of coriander/ cilantro leaves, chopped
1 handful of mint leaves, chopped

TO SERVE
1 recipe quantity Boiled Long-Grain Rice (*see page 237*)

Cashew nuts have a delicate flavour that complements all the different spices in this delicious curry, and they also create a really smooth and creamy sauce. This dish is a genuine classic Sri Lankan dish that is served with other curries, and is usually included on the menu for special occasions.

1 Heat a heavy-based frying pan over a medium-high heat. Add the ground coriander, cumin and turmeric and dry-fry for 1–2 minutes until fragrant. Remove from the heat and leave to one side.

2 Heat the oil in a large saucepan over a medium-high heat. Add the onion and stir-fry for 2–3 minutes until soft and translucent. Tip in the lemongrass stalks and cinnamon stick and stir-fry for 1 minute, then add the ginger and garlic and stir-fry for 2 minutes, or until fragrant. Stir in the toasted spice powder, chilli powder and pepper, then toss through the cashew nuts until well coated with the spices.

3 Pour in the coconut milk and 115ml/3¾fl oz/scant ½ cup water. Bring to the boil, then reduce the heat to low, cover and simmer for 15 minutes, stirring occasionally.

4 Add the sugar and salt, stir to mix well, then continue to simmer for a further 15 minutes until the cashew nuts start to soften. Sprinkle over the coriander and mint and serve hot with boiled rice.

AUBERGINE CURRY

SERVES 4
PREPARATION TIME 15 minutes, plus 30 minutes resting time
COOKING TIME 25 minutes

250g/9oz baby aubergines/ eggplants or large aubergine/eggplant
2 tbsp sunflower oil
½ tsp black mustard seeds
1 onion, chopped
1 recipe quantity Aubergine Curry Spice Paste (*see page 226*)
100g/3½oz sweet potato, peeled and cut into small cubes
1 tbsp lime juice
sea salt

TO SERVE
Garlic Naan (*see page 196*)

Aubergine is a great choice for a curry because, when cooked, it becomes very soft and tender. Its unique flavour goes particularly well in this recipe, as it acts like a sponge and absorbs the spicy sauce. If you can get them, baby aubergines, which are slim and oblong in shape, are great in this dish because of their softer texture when cooked.

1 Cut the baby aubergines in half lengthways or the large aubergine in slices about 1cm/½in thick, then arrange on a tray, cut sides facing up, and generously sprinkle with salt. Leave to stand for 30 minutes, then rinse under running cold water and pat dry with paper towels. Leave to one side.

2 Heat the oil in a large, deep, heavy-based frying pan. Add the mustard seeds and sizzle for a few seconds, then add the onion and stir-fry for 2–3 minutes until soft and translucent. Add the spice paste and cook gently, stirring occasionally, for 5–7 minutes until fragrant.

3 Tip the aubergine and sweet potato into the pan, toss until well coated with the paste, then cook, stirring occasionally, for 5 minutes until they start to soften. Add the lime juice and 55ml/1¾fl oz/scant ¼ cup water and season with salt. Reduce the heat to low and cook, covered, for 10 minutes until the aubergine and sweet potato are soft. Serve hot with the Garlic Naan.

MASALA DOSA

My love of Indian food started when I was eight years old and my mum served me my first Roti Canai (*see page 128*). One of my all-time favourites now is Masala Dosa – crispy roti wrapped with masala squash and served with any kind of curry sauce and chutney you like.

MAKES **about 8**
PREPARATION TIME **20 minutes,** plus soaking the dhal and rice overnight and 3–4 hours fermenting time
COOKING TIME **30–45 minutes**

1 tbsp sunflower oil, plus extra for oiling
½ tsp black mustard seeds
2 sprigs curry leaves
1 small butternut squash, deseeded, peeled and diced
2 carrots, diced
½ tsp ground coriander
¼ tsp ground cumin
½ tsp ground turmeric
¼ tsp chilli powder
sea salt and freshly ground black pepper

DOSA
80g/2¾oz/½ cup split white urad dhal, washed and soaked overnight
150g/5½oz/¾ cup basmati rice, washed and soaked overnight
¼ tsp chilli powder

TO SERVE
Dhal Curry (*see page 128 – optional*)
Sambal (*see page 236*)
plain yogurt

1 To make the dosa batter, drain and rinse the soaked urad dhal and basmati rice under running cold water, drain again and put in a food processor or blender. Blitz for a few seconds, then gradually pour in 290ml/10fl oz/generous 1 cup water until a smooth paste forms. Transfer the mixture to a bowl, add the chilli powder and season with salt and pepper. Cover with cling film/plastic wrap and leave to stand at room temperature for 3–4 hours for the batter to ferment.

2 Heat the oil in a frying pan over a medium-high heat. Add the mustard seeds and curry leaves and sizzle for a few seconds, then add the butternut squash and carrots and cook, stirring occasionally, for 7–8 minutes until they start to soften. Add the coriander, cumin, turmeric and chilli powder and season with salt and pepper. Pour 150ml/5fl oz/scant ⅔ cup water into the pan and bring to the boil. Reduce the heat to low and cook, covered, for 15–20 minutes until the squash and carrots are softened. Set aside and keep warm.

3 Meanwhile, pour some oil into a large, non-stick frying pan or crêpe pan over a medium-high heat, then use a paper towel to grease the pan evenly and soak up any excess oil. When the pan is hot, ladle about 55ml/1¾fl oz/scant ¼ cup of the dosa batter into the pan and use the base of the ladle to spread the mixture out as evenly as possible, using a circular motion, until about 23cm/9in in diameter. Cook for 2–3 minutes on each side until golden brown and crisp around the edges.

4 Transfer the dosa to a clean surface and put 2–3 tablespoons of the butternut squash mixture in the centre and mould into an oblong shape. Fold the dosa in half over the mixture, then transfer to a serving plate and keep warm. Repeat until all the batter is used. Serve immediately with Dhal Curry, sambal and yogurt if you like.

Beef & Vegetable Roti Parcels

MAKES **14**
PREPARATION TIME **30 minutes,
  plus 1 hour resting time**
COOKING TIME **about 1 hour**

200g/7oz sweet potatoes,
  diced
150g/5½oz floury potatoes,
  diced
1 tbsp sunflower oil, plus
  extra for oiling
1 onion, finely chopped
1 sprig curry leaves, finely
  chopped
1 tsp ground cumin
1 tsp ground coriander
½ tsp chilli powder
¼ tsp ground turmeric
1 small carrot, cut into
  matchsticks
2 spring onions/scallions,
  finely chopped
250g/9oz minced/ground
  beef
sea salt and freshly ground
  black pepper

ROTI DOUGH
½ tsp sea salt
150ml/5fl oz/scant ⅔ cup
  water
250g/9oz/2 cups plain/
  all-purpose flour
1 tbsp sunflower oil, plus
  extra for kneading and
  oiling

TO SERVE
chilli sauce (optional)

1 To make the roti dough, dissolve the salt in water. Put the flour in a
  large mixing bowl, make a well in the centre and add the oil. Slowly
  pour in the salted water and combine with the other ingredients to
  form a soft dough. Knead for 10 minutes, or until the dough is smooth
  and elastic, then shape into a ball. Cover with cling film/plastic wrap
  and leave to stand at room temperature for about 30 minutes.

2 Bring a saucepan of well-salted water to the boil. Tip in both the
  sweet and floury potatoes and cook for 10–15 minutes until soft.
  Drain well, then roughly mash with a fork and set aside.

3 Meanwhile, heat the oil in a frying pan over a medium-high heat. Add
  the onion and stir-fry for 2–3 minutes until soft and translucent. Add
  the curry leaves and ground spices and stir-fry for about 1 minute.
  Add the carrot and spring onions and cook for 5 minutes, or until the
  carrots are tender, stirring occasionally. Add the beef, break up any
  lumps and then add 2 tablespoons water. Season, then cook for 5–7
  minutes until cooked through, stirring occasionally. Stir in the mashed
  potatoes, then remove the pan from the heat and leave to one side.

4 Turn the dough onto a lightly oiled surface and knead for 5 minutes.
  Divide into 14 portions and shape into balls. Brush generously with
  oil, then place side by side on a well-oiled dish. Cover with cling film/
  plastic wrap and leave to stand at room temperature for 30 minutes.

5 Oil a clean working surface and generously oil your palms. Take a
  dough ball and flatten, then slowly work the dough outwards from
  around the edge until the circle is about 14–16cm/5½–6¼in in
  diameter. Place 2 tablespoons of the potato mixture in the centre
  of the pastry, slightly flatten the mixture and mould into an oblong
  shape about 1.5cm/⅝in thick. Fold the bottom edge of the pastry
  over the filling, fold in the two sides and roll up tightly. Transfer to
  a lightly oiled plate and repeat until all the dough balls are used.

6 Lightly oil a large, non-stick frying pan and place over a medium-
  high heat. Fry 4–5 rotis at a time for 8–10 minutes until crisp and
  brown all round, then turn the rotis upright and fry each end for
  2–3 minutes until brown spots form. Remove from the pan and
  keep warm. Repeat until all the rotis are cooked. Serve hot with
  chilli sauce on the side, if you like.

SERVES **4**
PREPARATION TIME **20 minutes**
COOKING TIME **25 minutes**

1 tbsp sunflower oil
1 onion, roughly chopped
2 garlic cloves, chopped
1 green chilli, deseeded and
    roughly chopped
180g/6¼oz white cabbage,
    core removed and roughly
    chopped
1 carrot, cut into matchsticks
400g/14oz skinless,
    boneless chicken thighs,
    cut into strips (or use
    leftover cooked/roast
    chicken meat)
½ tsp ground coriander
¼ tsp ground cumin
½ tsp ground turmeric
¼ tsp chilli powder
300g/10½oz roti, roughly
    chopped
sea salt

CHICKEN KOTTU ROTI

This is probably one of the tastiest Sri Lankan street foods, which makes great use of easy-to-source ingredients. If you have some leftovers from the day before, it is definitely a good idea to clear your refrigerator. You can substitute the protein and if you have made Roti Canai (*see page 128*), you can use that, otherwise store-bought roti canai/paratha are fine, too. Tortillas are a great substitute if you can't find roti.

1 Heat the oil in a wok or frying pan over a medium-high heat. Add the onion and garlic and stir-fry for 1–2 minutes until fragrant but not coloured. Tip in the chilli, cabbage and carrot and stir-fry for 5 minutes.

2 Add the chicken, coriander, cumin, turmeric and chilli powder, season with salt and cook for about 2–3 minutes. Pour in 100ml/3½fl oz/scant ½ cup of water, stir to combine and slowly bring to the boil.

3 Add the roti, stir until well combined and cook for a further 5–7 minutes or until the liquid is soaked up by all the ingredients. Serve hot.

GULAB JAMUN

These dough balls are a very well known and classic Indian dessert and are deliciously sweet as they soak up the fragrant sticky syrup. They are as addictive as they look, creating a perfect dessert for any special occasion or festive season.

SERVES **4**
PREPARATION TIME **25 minutes,**
  plus 1 hour soaking time
COOKING TIME **30 minutes**

200g/7oz/1 cup caster/
  granulated sugar
4 green cardamom pods,
  lightly crushed
a pinch of saffron threads
200g/7oz dried milk powder
100g/3½oz/¾ cup plain/
  all-purpose flour
½ tsp bicarbonate of soda/
  baking soda
100ml/3½fl oz/scant ½ cup
  buttermilk, plus extra if
  needed
500ml/17fl oz/2 cups
  sunflower oil, for
  deep-frying

TO SERVE
1 tbsp chopped pistachio
  nuts

1 To make the sugar syrup, put the sugar, cardamom pods, saffron threads and 100ml/3½fl oz/scant ½ cup of water in a saucepan. Bring to the boil over a medium-high heat, stirring constantly to dissolve the sugar, then reduce the heat to medium-low and boil gently for about 5–6 minutes or until the mixture starts to thicken, turning to almost like cordial-style syrup. Remove the cardamom pods and then everything from the heat and leave to one side.

2 Sift the milk powder, flour and bicarbonate of soda into a bowl, then tip in the buttermilk and mix until well combined to form a soft, sticky dough. Add a little more buttermilk if the dough seems crumbly. Take a small portion and shape into a small ball of 3cm/1¼in in diameter. Place the ball on a plate, then continue until all the dough has been used. You will get between 14–16 balls.

3 Heat the oil in a deep, heavy saucepan to 180°C/350°F, or until a small piece of bread turns brown in 15 seconds. Fry the balls in 2 batches to avoid overcrowding, as this will lower the temperature of the oil. First fry for about 2 minutes, then after 2 minutes, reduce the heat to low and fry until golden brown. Keep stirring gently to give them even colour. Remove from the oil, using a slotted spoon and drain on paper towels. Repeat with the remaining balls, bringing the oil back up to temperature between each batch.

4 Once the deep-fried dough balls are cool, divide them into individual bowls, pour over the cooled syrup, dividing it evenly between each portion, and leave to soak for about 1 hour. Decorate with the chopped pistachio nuts, just before serving.

SRI LANKAN CRISPY PANCAKES

Hoppers, also known as Appam, are eaten in Sri Lanka at breakfast, lunch and dinner. They are cooked in a special pan that looks like a mini wok, giving them a curvy shape when cooked. If you don't have a hopper pan, you can improvise by using either a small non-stick frying pan or the bottom section of a wok. Hoppers can be made in a variety of different ways, both sweet and savoury, and the egg hopper is one very popular example. Here I have included a recipe for a plain hopper, but I have included instructions on how to make simple sweet hoppers and egg hoppers, too. Because of their simple flavour and crispy outer layer, plain hoppers are great with curries.

MAKES **12**
PREPARATION TIME **10 minutes,** plus 2 hours resting time
COOKING TIME **about 1 hour**

PLAIN HOPPERS
2 tsp granulated sugar
½ tsp sea salt
2¼ tsp dried active yeast
500ml/17fl oz/2 cups coconut milk
350g/12oz/2 cups rice flour
2 eggs
sunflower oil, for oiling

SWEET HOPPERS
granulated or soft light brown sugar, to taste
shredded fresh coconut or desiccated/dried shredded coconut, to taste

EGG HOPPERS
12 eggs

1 Mix the sugar, salt and yeast in the coconut milk until dissolved. Put the rice flour in a large mixing bowl, make a well in the centre and crack the eggs into the well. Gradually add the coconut milk mixture, whisking continuously to form a smooth batter. Cover with cling film/plastic wrap and leave to stand in a warm place for 2 hours.

2 Pour some oil into a hopper pan or 16cm/6¼in heavy-based frying pan over a medium-high heat, then use a paper towel to grease the pan evenly and soak up any excess oil. When the pan is hot, ladle about 80ml/2½fl oz/⅓ cup of the batter into the centre of the pan and quickly lift and swirl the pan to form a thin layer over the base and as far up the sides of the pan as possible to create a shallow bowl shape. Cover the pan, reduce the heat to medium and cook for 3–4 minutes until the edges start to brown and bubbles start to form on the surface. The pancake should be crispy on the outside and slightly spongy in the middle. Transfer the hopper to a serving plate and keep warm, then repeat until all the batter is used.

3 To make sweet hoppers, sprinkle sugar and coconut, to taste, over the plain hopper halfway through cooking. Serve immediately.

4 To make egg hoppers, crack an egg into the centre of each hopper after 1–2 minutes of cooking or when the batter starts to thicken and set. Continue to cook, still covered, for 1–2 minutes until the egg white turns solid and opaque. Serve immediately.

BASIC RECIPES

Within the main recipes you will often find cross-references to spice pastes, condiments, rice and noodles that will be either a key part of the recipe or a suggested accompaniment to the dish. All the recipes, including my fool-proof method to boil rice, can be found here. Each paste recipe makes the exact quantity you will need in the recipe, and takes 5–10 minutes to make, plus any soaking time required. A mortar and pestle can be used instead of a food processor to blend the pastes, if you prefer.

SPICE PASTES

AUBERGINE CURRY SPICE PASTE

3 dried chillies • 2 red chillies, deseeded and roughly chopped • 3 garlic cloves, roughly chopped • 5 shallots, roughly chopped • 1cm/½in piece of fresh ginger, peeled and roughly chopped • ¼ tsp ground turmeric • ½ tsp ground coriander • ½ tsp ground cumin

1 Soak the dried chillies in hot water for 10 minutes, then drain, deseed and roughly chop. Put all the chillies, garlic, shallots and ginger in a food processor and blend into a smooth paste. Add the turmeric, coriander and cumin and mix well.

AYAM MASAK MERAH SPICE PASTE

3 dried chillies • 10 shallots, roughly chopped • 4 garlic cloves, roughly chopped • 2cm/¾in piece of fresh ginger, peeled and roughly chopped • 3 red chillies, deseeded and roughly chopped

1 Soak the dried chillies in hot water for 10 minutes, then drain, deseed and roughly chop. Put all the ingredients in a food processor and blend to a smooth paste.

ASSAM LAKSA SPICE PASTE

4 dried chillies • 6 red chillies, deseeded and roughly chopped • 1 tsp roasted shrimp paste (*see page 242*) • 10 shallots, roughly chopped • 1 lemongrass stalk, outer leaves and stalk end removed and roughly chopped

1 Soak the dried chillies in hot water for 10 minutes, then drain, deseed and roughly chop. Put all the ingredients in a food processor and blend to a smooth paste.

CHILLI CRAB SPICE PASTE

2 dried chillies • 5 red chillies, deseeded and roughly chopped • 2 garlic cloves, roughly chopped • 6 shallots, roughly chopped • 5cm/2in piece of fresh ginger, peeled and roughly chopped • 1 tsp roasted shrimp paste (*see page 242*)

1 Soak the dried chillies in hot water for 10 minutes, then drain, deseed and roughly chop. Put all the ingredients in a food processor and blend to a smooth paste.

COORG-Style CURRY SPICe PASte

2 green chillies, deseeded and roughly chopped •
1 red onion, roughly chopped • 3 garlic cloves,
roughly chopped • 1cm/½in piece of fresh ginger,
peeled and roughly chopped • ¼ tsp black
peppercorns • ½ tsp ground cumin • 1 tsp ground
coriander

1 Soak the dried chillies in hot water for 10
   minutes, then drain, deseed and roughly chop.
   Put all the ingredients, except the cumin and
   coriander, in a food processor and blend to a
   smooth paste. Add the cumin and coriander and
   mix well.

CURRY FISH MOUSSE SPICE PASte

1 red chilli, deseeded and roughly chopped • 2 garlic
cloves, roughly chopped • 5 shallots, roughly
chopped • 2 lemongrass stalks, outer leaves and stalk
ends removed and roughly chopped • 1cm/½in piece
of fresh turmeric, peeled and roughly chopped, or
½ tsp ground turmeric • 2cm/¾in piece of galangal,
peeled and roughly chopped • 2 kaffir lime leaves,
roughly chopped

1 Put all the ingredients, except the ground
   turmeric, if using, in a food processor and blend
   to a smooth paste. Add the ground turmeric
   and mix well.

COtO MAKASSAR SPICe PASte

3 green chillies, deseeded and roughly chopped •
2 red chillies, deseeded and roughly chopped •
3cm/1¼in piece of fresh ginger, peeled and roughly
chopped • 3 garlic cloves, roughly chopped •
80g/2¾oz coriander/cilantro leaves, roughly chopped
• 1 tsp ground coriander • ½ tsp ground turmeric

1 Put all the ingredients, except the ground
   coriander and turmeric, in a food processor and
   blend to a smooth paste. Add the coriander
   and turmeric and mix well.

GADO GADO SPICe PASte

3 red chillies, deseeded and roughly chopped • 3
garlic cloves, roughly chopped • 5 shallots, roughly
chopped • 2cm/¾in piece of fresh ginger, peeled
and roughly chopped • 1 lemongrass stalk, outer
leaves and stalk end removed and roughly chopped
• 1 tsp roasted shrimp paste (*see page 242*)

1 Blend all the ingredients in a food processor to
   a smooth paste.

KHMER YELLOW CURRY SPICE PASTE

1 red chilli, deseeded and roughly chopped • 4 garlic cloves, roughly chopped • 5 shallots, roughly chopped • 2 lemongrass stalks, outer leaves and stalk ends removed and roughly chopped • 3 kaffir lime leaves, roughly chopped • 2cm/¾in piece of galangal, peeled and roughly chopped • 2cm/¾in piece of fresh turmeric, peeled and roughly chopped, or 1 tsp ground turmeric

1 Put all the ingredients, except the ground turmeric, if using, in a food processor and blend to a smooth paste. Add the ground turmeric and mix well.

LAKSA SPICE PASTE

10 dried chillies • 5 red chillies, deseeded and roughly chopped • 6 garlic cloves, roughly chopped • 18 shallots, roughly chopped • 1 lemongrass stalk, outer leaves and stalk end removed and roughly chopped • 2cm/¾in piece of fresh ginger, peeled and roughly chopped • 1 tsp roasted shrimp paste (*see page 244*) • 2 macadamia nuts • 4cm/1½in piece of fresh turmeric, peeled and roughly chopped, or 2 tsp ground turmeric • 1 tbsp ground coriander • 1 tsp ground cumin

1 Soak the dried chillies in hot water for 10 minutes, then drain, deseed and roughly chop. Put all the ingredients, except the ground turmeric, if using, coriander and cumin, in a food processor and blend to a smooth paste. Add the ground turmeric, coriander and cumin and mix well.

KARE KARE SPICE PASTE

2 red chillies, deseeded and roughly chopped • 4 garlic cloves, roughly chopped • 8 shallots, roughly chopped • 2cm/¾in piece of fresh ginger, peeled and roughly chopped • 1 tsp roasted shrimp paste (*see page 242*)

1 Blend all the ingredients in a food processor to a smooth paste.

PAJERI NANAS SPICE PASTE

3 dried chillies • 6 red chillies, deseeded and roughly chopped • 3 garlic cloves, roughly chopped • 10 shallots, roughly chopped • 1cm/½in piece of fresh ginger, peeled and roughly chopped

1 Soak the dried chillies in hot water for 10 minutes, then drain, deseed and roughly chop. Put all the ingredients in a food processor and blend to a smooth paste.

PANANG CURRY SPICE PASTE

8 dried chillies • 2 red chillies, deseeded and roughly chopped • 1 tsp roasted shrimp paste (*see page 244*) • 2 garlic cloves, roughly chopped • 4 shallots, roughly chopped • 1 lemongrass stalk, outer leaves and stalk end removed and roughly chopped • 3cm/1¼in piece of galangal, peeled and roughly chopped • 2 kaffir lime leaves, roughly chopped • 2 coriander/cilantro roots with stalks, roughly chopped • 1 tsp ground coriander • ½ tsp ground cumin

1 Soak the dried chillies in hot water for 10 minutes, then drain, deseed and roughly chop. Put all the ingredients, except the ground coriander and cumin, in a food processor and blend to a smooth paste. Add the coriander and cumin to the paste and mix well.

SATE LILIT IKAN SPICE PASTE

5 red chillies, deseeded and roughly chopped • 4 garlic cloves, roughly chopped • 8 shallots, roughly chopped • 3cm/1¼in piece of fresh ginger, peeled and roughly chopped • 1 lemongrass stalk, outer leaves and stalk end removed and roughly chopped • 3 kaffir lime leaves, roughly chopped • 2 macadamia nuts • 1 tsp roasted shrimp paste (*see page 242*) • 1cm/½in piece of fresh turmeric, peeled and roughly chopped, or ½ tsp ground turmeric • 1 tsp ground coriander

1 Put all the ingredients, except the ground turmeric, if using, and coriander in a food processor and blend to a smooth paste. Add the ground turmeric and coriander and mix well.

RENDANG SPICE PASTE

8 dried chillies • 4 red chillies, deseeded and roughly chopped • 5 garlic cloves, roughly chopped • 1 red onion, roughly chopped • 10 shallots, roughly chopped • 1 lemongrass stalk, outer leaves and stalk end removed and roughly chopped • 2cm/¾in piece of fresh ginger, peeled and roughly chopped • 2cm/¾in piece of galangal, peeled and roughly chopped • 2cm/¾in piece of fresh turmeric, peeled and roughly chopped, or 1 tsp ground turmeric • 1 tbsp ground coriander • 1 tsp ground cumin

1 Soak the dried chillies in hot water for 10 minutes, then drain, deseed and roughly chop. Put all the ingredients, except the ground turmeric, if using, coriander and cumin, in a food processor and blend to a smooth paste. Add the ground turmeric, coriander and cumin and mix well.

SOUR FISH CURRY SPICE PASTE

½ tsp ground turmeric • ½ tsp ground coriander • ½ tsp chilli powder • ¼ tsp ground cumin • ¼ tsp freshly ground black pepper • 3 shallots, roughly chopped • 2 garlic cloves, roughly chopped • 3 green chillies, deseeded and roughly chopped • 1cm/½in piece of fresh ginger, peeled and roughly chopped

1 Put the turmeric, coriander, chilli powder, cumin and black pepper in a frying pan over a medium-high heat and dry-fry for 1–2 minutes until fragrant and slightly smoky. Transfer to a mixing bowl. Put the shallots, garlic, green chillies and ginger in a food processor and blend to a smooth paste. Add the toasted spice powder and mix well.

SQUID SPICE PASTE

4 dried chillies • 5 red chillies, deseeded and roughly chopped • 3 garlic cloves, roughly chopped • 10 shallots, roughly chopped • 1 tsp roasted shrimp paste (*see page 242*) • 2 macadamia nuts

1 Soak the dried chillies in hot water for 10 minutes, then drain, deseed and roughly chop. Put all the ingredients in a food processor and blend to a smooth paste.

THAI GREEN CURRY SPICE PASTE

7 green chillies, deseeded and roughly chopped •
2 red bird's eye chillies, deseeded and roughly
chopped • 5 shallots, roughly chopped • 3 garlic
cloves, roughly chopped • 3cm/1¼in piece of
galangal, peeled and roughly chopped • 1 lemongrass
stalk, outer leaves and stalk end removed and roughly
chopped • 3 kaffir lime leaves, roughly chopped •
1 tsp roasted shrimp paste (*see page 242*) •
3 coriander/cilantro roots with stalks and leaves,
roughly chopped • 5mm/¼in piece of fresh turmeric,
peeled and roughly chopped, or ¼ tsp ground
turmeric

1 Put all the ingredients, except the ground
  turmeric, if using, in a food processor and blend
  to a smooth paste. Add the ground turmeric and
  mix well.

THAI ROAST CHICKEN SPICE PASTE

1 red chilli, deseeded and roughly chopped • 3
shallots, roughly chopped • 1 lemongrass stalk, outer
leaves and stalk end removed and roughly chopped •
2 coriander/cilantro roots with stalks, roughly
chopped • 2cm/¾in piece of fresh turmeric, peeled
and roughly chopped, or 1 tsp ground turmeric

1 Put all the ingredients, except the ground
  turmeric, if using, in a food processor and blend
  to a smooth paste. Add the ground turmeric and
  mix well.

THAI RED CURRY SPICE PASTE

8 dried chillies • 2 red chillies, deseeded and roughly
chopped • 2 garlic cloves, roughly chopped •
4 shallots, roughly chopped • ½ lemongrass stalk,
outer leaves and stalk end removed and roughly
chopped • 3cm/1¼in piece of galangal, peeled and
roughly chopped • 1 tsp roasted shrimp paste (*see
page 242*) • 2 coriander/cilantro roots with stalks,
roughly chopped • 2 kaffir lime leaves, roughly
chopped

1 Soak the dried chillies in hot water for 10 minutes,
  then drain, deseed and roughly chop. Put all the
  ingredients in a food processor and blend to a
  smooth paste.

STOCKS

CHICKEN STOCK

800g/1lb 12oz chicken wings and drumsticks, skin and excess fat removed, or 1 x 1.5kg/3lb 5oz chicken carcass • 5cm/2in piece of fresh ginger, peeled and finely chopped • 6 spring onions/scallions, cut in half lengthways • 5 garlic cloves, chopped • ¼ tsp white peppercorns • 1 star anise • 2 tbsp Shaoxing rice wine

1 Put the chicken, ginger, spring onions, garlic, white peppercorns, star anise and rice wine in a large saucepan over a medium-high heat. Add 2 litres/70fl oz/8 cups water and bring to the boil. Reduce the heat to low, cover and simmer for 2–3 hours, skimming off any scum from the surface as required.

2 Remove the pan from the heat and discard all the solid ingredients. Cool the stock, then strain over a bowl lined with muslin/cheesecloth. Chicken stock can be frozen for up to 1 month.

PORK STOCK

300g/10½oz chicken wings and drumsticks, skin and excess fat removed • 500g/1lb 2oz pork ribs or pork bones • 5cm/2in piece of fresh ginger, peeled and finely chopped • 3 spring onions/scallions, cut in half lengthways • 5 garlic cloves, finely chopped • ¼ tsp white peppercorns

1 Put the chicken pieces, pork ribs, ginger, spring onions, garlic, white peppercorns and 2 litres/70fl oz/8 cups water in a large saucepan and bring to the boil. Reduce the heat to low and simmer for 2–3 hours, skimming off any scum from the surface as required.

2 Remove the pan from the heat and discard all the solid ingredients. Cool the stock, then strain over a bowl lined with muslin/cheesecloth. Pork stock can be frozen for up to 1 month.

DASHI

12cm/4½in kombu • 25g/1oz dried bonito flakes

1 Wipe the kombu with damp paper towels to remove any powder residue. Put the kombu in a saucepan and add 1.25 litres/44fl oz/5 cups water. Leave to sit for 30 minutes. Place the saucepan over a medium-low heat, bring to the boil and then remove the kombu. Reduce the heat to low, add the bonito flakes, cover and simmer for about 5 minutes.

2 Remove the pan from the heat and let the bonito flakes sink to the bottom. Skim off any scum from the surface, then strain the stock over a bowl lined with muslin/cheesecloth. Leave the dashi to cool. This is Ichiban Dashi, which is the first stock with a more intense flavour.

3 You can reuse the kombu and bonito flakes to make Niban Dashi, which is the second stock with a milder flavour. Use the same amount of water as above and simmer all the ingredients for about 10 minutes. Strain the stock through muslin as above and discard the solids. Dashi can be frozen for up to 1 month.

condiments & sides

CHILLI OIL

300ml/10½fl oz/scant 1¼ cups sunflower oil • 1 cinnamon stick, about 5cm/2in long • 1 star anise • 150g/5½oz/¾ cup chilli flakes • 1 tsp Sichuan peppercorns, crushed

1 Heat the oil in a deep, heavy-based frying pan to about 160°C/315°F or until a small piece of bread turns brown in 25–30 seconds. Add the cinnamon stick and star anise and fry for 1–2 minutes, stirring occasionally, until fragrant. Remove and discard the cinnamon stick and star anise.

2 Make sure the oil is still hot, but no hotter, and add the chilli flakes. Stir for a few seconds, then remove the pan from the heat.

3 Leave the oil and chilli flakes to cool and then transfer to a sterilized preserving jar or bottle. The chilli oil can be kept in the refrigerator for many weeks.

CHILLI PASTE

50g/1¾oz dried chillies • 3 tbsp sunflower oil • 1 tbsp sugar • ½ tsp salt

1 Soak the dried chillies in hot water for 10–15 minutes, then drain, deseed and roughly chop. Put the chillies in a food processor and blend to a smooth paste.

2 Heat the oil in a frying pan over a medium-high heat. Add the chilli paste and cook gently, stirring occasionally, for 15–20 minutes until fragrant and the oil starts to rise to the surface. Stir in the sugar and salt, remove from the heat and cool. Chilli paste can be frozen for up to 2 months.

FRIED SHALLOTS

250ml/9fl oz/1 cup sunflower oil • 350g/12oz red shallots, thinly sliced

1 Heat the oil in a frying pan over a medium heat. Insert a chopstick into the oil to test if it is hot enough – bubbles will start to form around the chopstick. Add the shallots and fry, stirring occasionally, for about 5–7 minutes until golden brown. Using a slotted spoon, remove the shallots from the pan and drain in a fine sieve over a mixing bowl, then on paper towels to soak up any excess oil.
2 Reuse the oil for cooking, if you like. Cool, then store in an airtight container in a cool, dark place for later use for up to 1 week.

GROUND TOASTED SICHUAN PEPPER

50g/1¾oz/¼ cup Sichuan peppercorns

1 Heat a frying pan over a medium-low heat. Add the Sichuan peppercorns and dry-fry for 5 minutes, or until fragrant – be careful they don't burn.
2 Remove from the heat and leave to cool. Grind the peppercorns in a food processor or coffee grinder and store in a cool, dark place in an airtight jar for up to 1 month.

NAM PRIK PAO

50g/1¾oz dried chillies, rinsed • 30g/1oz dried shrimps, rinsed • 125ml/4fl oz/½ cup sunflower oil • 30g/1oz garlic cloves, sliced • 100g/3½oz shallots, sliced • 1 tsp roasted shrimp paste (*see page 244*) • 2 tbsp fish sauce • 1 recipe quantity Tamarind Water (*see page 244*)

1 Heat a frying pan over a medium-high heat. Add the dried chillies and dry-fry for 2–3 minutes until slightly smoky. Remove from the pan and set aside. Make sure your kitchen is well ventilated because the smell can be very pungent.
2 Using the same pan, lightly fry the dried shrimps for 2–3 minutes until fragrant and the colour changes. Leave to one side to cool.
3 Meanwhile, heat the oil in a deep frying pan or wok over a medium heat. Add the garlic and shallots and fry, stirring occasionally, for 5–7 minutes until lightly golden brown. Using a slotted spoon, remove the shallots and garlic from the oil. Leave the frying pan, with the oil, for later use.
4 Once the shallots and garlic are cool, put in a food processor with the dried chillies, toasted dried shrimps and roasted shrimp paste and blend to a slightly coarse paste.
5 Reheat the oil in the frying pan over a medium-low heat. Add the chilli paste and cook gently, stirring occasionally, for 5 minutes, or until fragrant and the colour has darkened. Mix in the fish sauce and tamarind water. Transfer the paste to a preserving jar and cool. Store in the refrigerator for up to 1 month.

NUOC CHAM DIPPING SAUCE

1 garlic clove, finely chopped • 1 tsp chopped red bird's eye chilli • 2 tbsp caster/superfine sugar • 5 tbsp lime juice • 2 tbsp fish sauce

1 Put all the ingredients into a bowl, add 2 tablespoons water and stir until the sugar is dissolved.

PICKLED GINGER

500g/1lb 2oz fresh ginger • 1 tbsp salt • 350ml/12fl oz/scant 1½ cups rice vinegar • 250g/9oz/scant 1¼ cups granulated sugar

1 Cut the ginger into small pieces for easier handling. Hold the ginger firmly in one hand and scrape off the peel using a spoon or a small, sharp knife. Slice the ginger into thin 2mm/¹⁄₁₆in pieces.
2 Put the ginger in a colander and rub with the salt to draw out the moisture. Leave to sit in the colander for about 1 hour, then rinse thoroughly under running cold water. Squeeze out any excess liquid and pat dry with paper towels. Transfer the ginger to a large preserving jar.
3 Put the rice vinegar and sugar in a saucepan over a medium-high heat. Bring to the boil, stirring continuously until the sugar is dissolved. Pour the liquid over the ginger and leave it to cool.
4 Cover and refrigerate for 24–36 hours before using. Pickled ginger can be stored in the refrigerator for up to 1 month.

SAMBAL

2 tsp roasted shrimp paste (*see page 244*) • 5 red chillies, deseeded and roughly chopped • 3 green bird's eye chillies, deseeded and roughly chopped • 2 tsp sugar • juice of 1 lime • ¼ tsp salt

1 Put the roasted shrimp paste and chillies in a food processor and blend to a smooth paste. Transfer to a mixing bowl, add the sugar, lime juice and salt and stir until the sugar is dissolved. Keep in a preserving jar in the refrigerator for up to 1 week.

SAMBAL MATAH

1 tsp roasted shrimp paste (*see page 244*) • 5 shallots, finely sliced • 2 garlic cloves, finely chopped • 2 red bird's eye chillies, deseeded and finely chopped • 2 kaffir lime leaves, finely chopped • 2 tsp sugar • 2 tbsp lime juice • a pinch of salt

1 Put all the ingredients in a bowl and mix until the sugar is dissolved and the paste well combined.

RICE

BOILED RICE

300g/10½oz/heaped 1⅓ cups short-grain rice or
350g/12oz/1¾ cups long-grain rice, such as jasmine
and basmati

1 Put the rice in a large saucepan and pour in
enough water to half fill the pan. Swirl the rice
using your hand, lightly rubbing the grains, until
the water is cloudy. Carefully pour off the water
and repeat this process 3 or 4 times until the
water is almost clear.

FOR BOILED SHORT-GRAIN RICE

2 Drain the rice into a sieve and leave to sit over a
bowl for about 10 minutes, then transfer the rice
to the saucepan and add 350ml/12fl oz/scant
1½ cups water. Leave to one side for about 20
minutes, then bring to the boil over a high heat
and give it a quick stir. Reduce the heat to low,
cover with a tight-fitting lid and simmer gently
for about 15 minutes, or until the liquid is
absorbed.
3 Remove the pan from the heat and then, using a
wooden or plastic spatula, quickly loosen the
grains. Replace the lid and leave the rice to steam
for 15 minutes until fluffy.

FOR BOILED LONG-GRAIN RICE

2 Cover the rice with water and leave to stand for
30 minutes. Drain the rice into a sieve and leave
to sit over a bowl for 10 minutes, then transfer
the rice to a saucepan and add 455ml/16fl oz/
scant 2 cups water. Place the pan over a high
heat and bring to the boil for about 20 seconds.
Stir the rice with a wooden spoon to prevent the
rice sticking to the base of the pan and then
reduce the heat to low, cover and simmer gently
for 20 minutes.
3 Remove the pan from the heat, leaving the lid
tightly closed, and leave to steam for 10–15
minutes until the rice is cooked. Fluff the rice
with a fork and keep warm.

BASIC techniques

COOKING EGG AND RICE NOODLES AND RICE STICKS

1 Prepare a large bowl of ice-cold water and place it next to the hob/stovetop. Fill a large saucepan with plenty of water and bring to the boil, then add the noodles or rice sticks and cook for the following times:

FRESH EGG NOODLES

2 Blanch for 25–30 seconds to warm through.

DRIED EGG NOODLES

2 Cook for 3–4 minutes until 'al dente'.

RICE STICKS

2 Cook for 2–3 minutes until 'al dente'.

DRIED RICE VERMICELLI

2 Cook for 2–3 minutes until 'al dente'.

THICK RICE NOODLES

2 Soak in boiling water for 30–45 minutes, then cook for 4–5 minutes until 'al dente'.
3 Using a noodle skimmer or kitchen tongs, remove the cooked noodles from the water and plunge for a few seconds into the ice-cold water. Meanwhile, bring the water in the pan back to the boil. Return the noodles to the boiling water for a few seconds to warm through, then drain and continue according to the recipe instructions.

COOKING SOBA NOODLES

1 Bring plenty of water to the boil in a large saucepan, add the soba noodles and cook for about 3–4 minutes or until al dente. If unsure if they are ready, take a bite from a strand of noodle – it should be cooked through completely without a hard core.
2 Drain the noodles and rinse under running cold water, swirling and gently rubbing the strands to remove the starch. Continue rinsing until the water runs clear.
3 Meanwhile, bring another saucepan of water to the boil. Plunge the cooked and rinsed soba noodles into the water for a few seconds to heat through, then drain and continue according to the recipe instructions.

DEBONING CHICKEN LEGS

1 Rinse the chicken legs under running cold water and pat dry with paper towels. Place one leg, skin-side down, on a chopping/cutting board and cut through the joint between the thigh and the drumstick using a large, sharp knife.
2 Take the thigh and make an incision along the top of the bone. Using quick, short strokes, deepen the incision to cut the meat away from the bone. Pull clear the top part of the bone and then continue to make a few more cuts to remove the bone completely. Cut off any small bits of bone, tendons, fat and skin.
3 Use the same process to remove the bone from the drumstick. Repeat for the remaining legs.

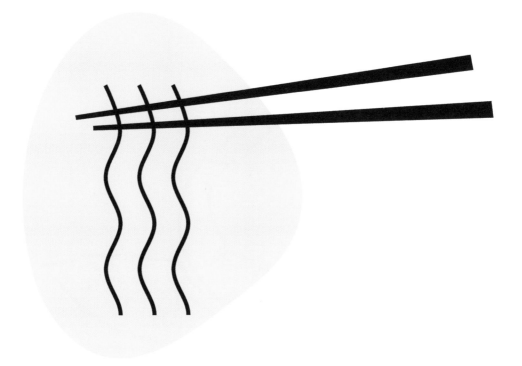

FRESHLY GRATED COCONUT

1 Insert a sharp metal skewer into the 'eyes' at the bottom of the coconut and drain out the juice. Preheat the oven to 180°C/350°F/Gas 4 and bake the coconut for about 15 minutes. Remove from the oven and leave to one side until cool enough to handle.

2 Using a hammer or cleaver, tap the middle of the coconut until cracks form, then break the coconut in two. If you have a coconut grater, use it to grate the coconut. If not, carefully slip a small, sharp knife between the shell and the flesh and pull the flesh away. Peel the brown skin off the back of the flesh using a vegetable peeler, then cut the flesh in chunks. Grate the flesh using a hand-held grater or blend it in a food processor to a desiccated/dried shredded coconut consistency.

FRESH COCONUT MILK

1 Grate the flesh, as above, and mix with 200ml/ 7fl oz/scant 1 cup water. Strain over a bowl lined with muslin/cheesecloth, squeezing out as much milk as possible. This is the 'first press'. It is thick and concentrated and is sometimes known as coconut cream. Set the milk aside while you extract the 'second press' coconut milk.

2 Add 45ml/1½fl oz/3 tbsp water to the grated coconut in the muslin and strain over a separate bowl, squeezing out as much milk as possible. It will have a much thinner consistency.

3 Unless a recipe specifically asks for coconut cream or second-press coconut milk, blend both the first- and second-press milks together. Coconut milk can be prepared in advance and can be frozen for up to 6 months.

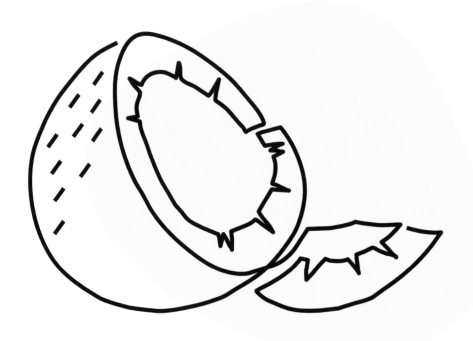

PREPARING PRAWNS

1 Hold the body of the prawn firmly, squeeze and pull off the head. Peel away the shell and legs from the body, then holding the body squeeze off the tail. Reserve the shell and head if using in a recipe – they are also great to flavour a stock.

2 To devein the prawn, hold it so the back of the prawn is slightly curved. Using a small knife, make a shallow incision along the back. Use a cocktail stick to remove the black vein.

3 If the prawns are to be used whole, make a few incisions vertically along the belly. This will prevent it from curling during cooking.

4 Rinse the prawns in running cold water and drain. Transfer the prawns to a deep bowl, add 1 tablespoon sea salt and use your hands to lightly massage the salt into the prawns. The use of salt at this stage is to give the prawns a springy texture. Rinse the prawns under running cold water, drain and pat dry with paper towels.

PREPARING SQUID

1 Place the squid on a chopping/cutting board and spread the tentacles out on the board. Cut off and discard the two longest tentacles.

2 Take the head in one hand and the body in the other and gently pull the head away from the body. It will take the intestines with it. Cut just in front of the eyes and remove and discard the eyes and intestines.

3 Next, pull out and discard the inedible beak from the base of the tentacles and the transparent silver quill found inside the body.

4 Finally, pull off the two fins on either side of the body and pull away the spotty skin from both the body and the fins. Discard the fins and use the tentacles, if you like. Thoroughly rinse the pieces of squid, inside and out, under running cold water, then pat dry with paper towels.

5 Squid can be cut into rings or scored with a diamond pattern. To do the latter, cut open the body by sliding a sharp, flexible knife into the opening of the body and along its entire length. Flatten the body out on a chopping/cutting board, inner surface facing up. Position your knife at 90° to the surface, then make very shallow diagonal crisscross cuts in the flesh. By scoring the squid on the inside surface, it will curl with the inside facing out when cooked. Cut the body into pieces according to the recipe instructions.

PREPARING BEEF TO BE THINLY SLICED

1 Rinse the beef under running cold water and pat dry with paper towels. Cover with cling film/plastic wrap and freeze for about 25 minutes, so that the beef is firm to the touch but not frozen solid.
2 Remove the beef from the freezer, unwrap the cling film/plastic wrap and place the beef on a chopping/cutting board. Using a sharp knife, cut the beef against the grain into 3mm/⅛in slices, or even thinner if possible.

REHYDRATING DRIED MUSHROOMS

1 Put the dried mushrooms in a bowl, pour over boiling water and soak for 20–25 minutes until soft. Drain off the liquid, straining the liquid into a clean bowl, if using, and squeeze off any excess liquid. Trim off the stems.

ROASTED SHRIMP PASTE

1 Put the recipe quantity of shrimp paste in the middle of a square piece of foil and break it into pieces with a spoon. Fold in the edges to form a small package and roast in a preheated oven at 200°C/400°F/Gas 6 for about 5 minutes. Remove and leave to one side to cool. The roasted shrimp will smell aromatic and be a darker-coloured dry powder.

SKINNING TOMATOES

1 Score the base of the tomato, put in a bowl and cover with boiling water. Leave to stand until the skin starts to curl, then drain off the water and fill the bowl with cold water. Leave to cool a little and remove the skin.

TAMARIND WATER

1 Put 50g/1¾oz tamarind pulp and 80ml/2½fl oz/ ⅓ cup boiling water in a small bowl. Soak for 30 minutes until soft. Use the back of a spoon to break the pulp into a pliable form, then strain through a fine sieve set over a bowl. Discard the solids.

TOASTED DRIED ANCHOVIES

1 Remove the heads and guts from the dried anchovies, then rinse under running cold water, drain and pat dry with paper towels.
2 Heat 1 teaspoon vegetable oil in a frying pan over a medium heat. Add the anchovies and toast until they turn golden brown.

GLOSSARY

BEAN CURD SHEET This is made from the layer of film that forms on the surface of soy milk when it is made. The film is collected and dried to become a translucent sheet.

BLACK BEAN PASTE Made from fermented and salted soybeans and with a pungent smell and bitter-sweet taste, black bean paste is often used in stir-fries.

BONITO FLAKES, DRIED Known as katsuobushi in Japanese, bonito flakes are dried, fermented and smoked skipjack tuna shavings that are commonly used in making dashi stock and miso soup.

CHILLI BEAN PASTE Also known as dou ban jiang in Chinese Mandarin. Chilli bean paste is made of chilli pepper, fermented soybeans, fermented broad beans and a mix of spices. It tastes both slightly spicy and salty at the same time.

CHINESE BLACK RICE VINEGAR Sometimes called Chinkiang vinegar, after the place it is produced, this vinegar tastes very similar to balsamic vinegar. It is often used in dipping sauces and in stir-fries.

CHINESE FIVE-SPICE This is a mix of five spices including black peppercorns, cloves, cinnamon, fennel seed and star anise. It is used in braised dishes and also to marinate meat. Ready-ground powder is readily available in the supermarket.

DAIKON Also known as Chinese radish or mooli in India, daikon is shaped like a very long carrot and has a mild flavour. It is often used in Japanese stews and as a pickle.

DRIED ANCHOVIES These are the small, salt-water fish that have been dried. Dried anchovies are often used in Korean cuisine as a stock base and are commonly used in sambal dishes in Malaysia and Indonesia. Most of the time, however, they are fried to give a crispy texture and added to salads or fried rice.

GALANGAL This is a rhizome from the ginger family. It has a pale yellow and pinkish skin and citrusy flavour. Galangal is normally used in curry pastes or to infuse stock.

GLUTINOUS RICE This is a type of short-grain rice that becomes very sticky once cooked. It is sometimes called sticky rice, and is normally soaked before steaming.

GLUTINOUS RICE FLOUR A highly absorbent flour made from glutinous rice. Often used to make Asian desserts, it becomes sticky, rubbery and chewy in texture.

HOISIN SAUCE This is commonly used as a condiment. It has a thick and sticky texture with a brown colour. It is made from soybeans, vinegar, sugar and other spices. It is a popular ingredient in marinades as it has a sweet and garlicky taste.

JERUSALEM ARTICHOKES Not related to the artichoke family, Jerusalem artichoke is a root vegetable that looks very like ginger. It has a sweet and nutty flavour and a crisp and crunchy texture, and can be eaten either raw or cooked.

JICAMA Also known as yam bean, jicama is a root vegetable that is commonly used in Southeast Asian and Central American cooking. It has a similar shape to the white round radish but it is bigger. Jicama has a crunchy texture and can be eaten raw and cooked. Substitutes are Jerusalem artichokes and water chestnuts.

KOMBU, DRIED An edible kelp that is widely used in Japanese cooking and, in the dried form, is one of the main ingredients in dashi.

KORean HOt PePPeR PASte Called gochujang in Korea, this paste is salty, spicy and pungent. It is made from Korean dried red pepper, fermented soybeans and other spices. It is normally used as a condiment, marinade or seasoning. It is almost equivalent to Chilli Bean Paste.

KORean ReD PePPeR POWDeR Called kochukara in Korea, this is a powder form of Korean dried red pepper. Korean red pepper is another variety of red chilli that is sun-dried. It is used in many Korean dishes such as kimchi and bulgogi.

Lotus Leaves From the lotus plant and used dried, the lotus leaf is a bright green colour. It is most often used to cook sticky rice in, to give it a more earthy and smoky flavour as well as to keep the ingredients moist.

MIRIN A Japanese sweet rice wine with a low alcohol content. It has a strong flavour, is very sweet and is often used instead of sugar.

NORI A dried sheet of seaweed, which is used to make sushi and sometimes as a garnish. It is slightly salty in flavour and has a crispy texture.

PALM SUGAR Widely used in Asian cooking, palm sugar is obtained from the sugary sap of certain palm trees. It usually comes in blocks, which you can chop or slice up, but is also found in granular and liquid form. If not available, replace with soft light brown sugar.

PANDAN LeAves Also known as screwpine leaves, pandan leaves are green, thin, long and pointed, and are used as a flavouring in savoury dishes and a colouring in desserts. When used as a flavouring in stocks or rice, they are normally tied into a knot for easy removal. Alternatively, they are snipped into pieces and then blended into a paste. The juice is then squeezed out and used. Pandan essence can be found in Asian supermarkets and is mostly used in making desserts.

SAGO PeARLS Sago is extracted from the pith of sago palm stems. Tiny white sago pearls are commonly used in Southeast Asia in desserts, and when cooked, turn translucent.

SAKe A popular alcoholic drink in Japan, sake is made from fermented rice. Because 'drinking' sake is quite expensive to be used in cooking, there is a cheaper cooking variety that can be found in Asian supermarkets.

SHOYU This is the Japanese version of light soy sauce, which has a richer and stronger flavour compared to Chinese light soy sauce. It is great in stir-fries, marinades or as a condiment.

SHRIMP PASte Shrimp paste is widely used in Southeast Asian cooking. It normally comes in a block and is made from fermented shrimp that is dried in the sun. It is known as belacan in Malay, terasi in Indonesian, kapi in Thai and khmer mam ruoc in Vietnamese. Uncooked shrimp paste is a bit sticky and has a pungent and strong fishy smell. Because of this, it is not advisable to toast shrimp paste in a pan in your kitchen, but to roast it in the oven instead (see page 242).

SICHUAN PePPeRCORNS They are reddish-brown in colour, have a very unique and strong flavour and are normally toasted before use in order to bring out the aroma.

TAMARIND PeeL This is made from sun-dried slices of the small, round, sour-tasting asam gelugor fruit grown on a tree native to Malaysia. It is also known as asam keping and not related to the tamarind fruit. Tamarind peel is mostly used in fish-based curries in Malaysia and Singapore.

TAMARIND PULP This is the sticky pulp taken from the inside of the tamarind pod. It is dark brown in colour and is normally sold in a block. The pulp needs to be soaked in warm water for about 30 minutes before use to make tamarind water (see page 242).

THAI BASIL The Thai basil leaf is long and pointed and the stem is purple. It has a much stronger and more pungent flavour than sweet basil and is normally used in salads, stir-fries and curry dishes.

VIETNAMESE CORIANDER LEAVES This is the most common name for polygonum leaves and is also known as Vietnamese mint as well as laksa leaves, or daun kesom in Malaysia and Singapore. They are normally used to infuse soup stock.

WAKAME This is a long, deep-green seaweed that usually comes in a dried form. A popular ingredient in Japanese cuisine, it is commonly used in salads or added to miso soup. Dried wakame has to be rehydrated in water before it can be used.

WASABI Also known as Japanese horseradish, wasabi has a very strong and fiery flavour. Once eaten, it stimulates the nasal passage, unlike chilli, which produces a hot sensation on the tongue. Wasabi is most commonly used as a condiment for sushi.

WATER CHESTNUTS An aquatic vegetable that is small and round. They can be eaten raw or cooked and the flesh has a crunchy texture.

WATER SPINACH Known as ong choi in China, this is a semi-aquatic vegetable with long, pointed leaves and a long, hollow stem. The texture is crunchy and it is normally used in stir-fries and soup dishes.

INDEX